Edited by KeNosha INK

Cover design by Jaiyde Simone

Book interior design by Masterpiece Kingdom Brands

TABLE OF CONTENTS

Hey, Friend!

What you thought would happen next,
is about to happen NOW!

ABOUT THE AUTHOR

Trinity Mitchell is a native of Mississippi. She hosts the well-known talk show, Friend Fusion. Friend Fusion is a platform that focuses on the power of relationships. After growing up in what she considers developmental circumstances, she established a passion for valuing people and relationships. In recent years, she took to social media to share her personal experiences and advice on relationships and eventually became known as, "Your Friend, Trin" on her popular Instagram account. Trin has a unique way of inspiring her friends all around the world to desire better for themselves and others by encouraging people to be accountable. Trin believes she is assigned to cancel the Cancel Culture by reaching one friend at a time. This book is her device to tell her friends that they don't have to wait until next time, next week or next year. If we make the right decisions NOW, the next can arrive sooner than we ever imagined.

FOREWORD

As a parent of four children ages 16, 13, 10, and 4, one of the most challenging things we do on a daily basis in our home is to provide a wake-up call for our children. Especially the older three. It's painful to go into their room and hear the peace, the sleep, the somber, the snoring, in the deepest of REM sleep. They are comatose, completely out of it. And then, we turn that light on. Oftentimes, we'll put on music and begin to say, "Wake up, wake up!" They begin to moan, slowly moving like large beasts in a forest, trying to figure out how to turn over and then stand up. Then the volume gets louder. We open up the window, the light gets brighter. We turn the music up higher. We call their names more often. "Get up, get up, get up!" And then they groan and moan and begin to sit up in their bed and open their eyes. Sometimes, they'll begin to exclaim, "I don't want to go to school, and I don't want to get up! I don't want to do anything!" This is the moment that feels like they are in their own little individual crisis. Like they are caught between sleep and waking up, between nothing and something, between no movement to full on activity. You could just see them fighting through this transition of waking up. It is painful. It is difficult. Sometimes there are tears. Sometimes there are temper tantrums.

Sometimes there's stomping. But it has to happen. It's inevitable that in order to start the day, you've got to go through the wake-up call. You've got to fight through the transition of being out of it and clueless, going from extremely comfortable to being engaged and being active. Getting to being about what the day demands of you, your life movement and activity.

As I think about it, this is something that we all have to learn to do in so many areas of our life. There are moments when we are challenged. There are moments when we are pushed out of our comfort and out of our slumber. There are areas where we're sleeping, those areas where we really need to be awake and engaged. There are areas where there's no activity when there really should be a lot of activity. The trauma of going through the wake-up call from no activity to activity, not being engaged, to being engaged in something, sometimes that trauma can be the most challenging thing. It can be the hardest thing to go through

There are three areas that are big wake-up calls that I hear ringing in the pages ahead. The first is a wake-up call to love yourself. To see you. To appreciate you, to acknowledge who you are, to love who you are, to value who you are, to respect and honor who you are, not based off of how you feel about you, not based off of what you think about you, but honestly, based off of what your creator thinks about you, what your creator feels about you, what your creator sees in you, allowing the one who made you to dictate the terms in which you are to operate and live. Loving yourself the way God sees you. If you struggle with loving yourself, you really should start acting like a thing is so, so that it might be so, because God said so.

The second area to experience a wake-up call is in the area of accountability. Loving yourself is one thing, but also loving the thing that makes you the best you is your ability to not only be accountable, but to also be held accountable. As an individual who desires more, being and doing better shouldn't be a cute idea. It certainly isn't something that happens overnight. The practice of submitting yourself to the will of God is hard and requires us to be completely surrendered to His plans rather than our own each and every day. Furthermore, taking care of yourself is not limited to how much exercise you do, how much water you drink, or how much weight you gain/lose. Taking care of yourself means you evolve physically, emotionally, and spiritually because you realize your ability to grow isn't predicated on your circumstances, but in your ability to make wise decisions that may yield delayed gratification. Accountability allows you to put together an intentional strategy, system, practices and rhythms around the instructions God has given you so you can perform and execute at the highest of levels.

The third area we need to experience a wake-up is in loving the people in your life. Loving good relationships. Answering the wake-up call to loving really good relationships and loving people well. One of your greatest assets in life will be your friendships. One of the most powerful, influential things in your life will be your relationships. And what does it mean to wake-up to the opportunity and the invitation to love relationships, to love people well, to be invested in relationships. Don't allow your life to move so fast, to where you miss opportunities to love hard, to love well, and to love long.

One of the most dangerous things about a wake-up call, especially with an alarm clock, is there's this snooze button. This snooze button gives you an opportunity to delay your awakening. It gives you an opportunity to delay getting up. Basically, what you say when you hit that snooze button is - not now, but later. Trinity Mitchell's words on the pages ahead serve as a powerful wake-up call. A wake-up call to love yourself, a wake-up call to love your health, a wake-up call to love relationships and honestly so much more. To sit with this book and to sit with her words will invite you to wake up to loving better, to being better, to living better. So, I encourage you don't hit the snooze button! This isn't for the next 10 minutes. This isn't for the next hour. This isn't for the next season. This is for now!

PRAISE FOR - REVIEWS

One thing about 2022, it presented me with so many opportunities and many obstacles. The constant battle of having to show up for myself and everyone else left me feeling tired and hopeless. When I received Trin's manuscript, it was just what I needed to put things into refreshing perspective. It is one thing to know God is able and another to experience His ability to do exceedingly, abundantly, and above all we could ask or think. *Now, Not Next* helped me make the decision that I'd not just know God exists, but He exists in and through me. My next is the new now because of your obedience, Trin. Much love and gratitude.

J Bolin,

Celebrity Fashion Stylist

PRAISE FOR - REVIEWS

After reading *Now, Not Next*, the comfort zone isn't comforting like it used to. As a husband, father, and pastor, I have fallen victim to meeting the expectations of others and not completing my own tasks. In this book, Trin defines what it means to finish. I have discovered that starting is actually the easiest part. However, relational assets, consistency, and accountability are necessary tools for finishing. If you truly desire to leave your now and enter into your next, start here with my friend, Trin.

Albert Tate

Lead Pastor of Fellowship Monrovia &Author

PRAISE FOR - REVIEWS

Now, Not Next is an excellent read. The author has a unique way of providing heavy, thought provoking content in an easily digestible manner. Trinity's "in your face because I'm your friend" approach to writing causes you to fall in love with her and her work. We've all been called to more as she reiterated throughout her book. But in order to live in this reality, one must properly navigate through the areas of life identified by the author as necessary for elevation. In so doing, what you thought is next can be your now. Well done, Trinity. Your hard work paid off here.

Dr. Kellie Agueze

Warrior Nation Ministries & Author

At this point in your life, what does transition mean to you?

CHAPTER 1

TRANSITION. We often use this word to reflect entering into different stages of life. "Transition" is defined as a process of change from a current condition to another. Even in death, Christians believe a transition exists from life on earth to eternal life. Ultimately, transition is inevitable and single-handedly one of the hardest things for most people to navigate their way through adulthood, parenthood, and, for some, childhood trauma. When I started writing this chapter, I thought I hadn't really experienced transition until I was a high school senior preparing for college, but as I continued to reflect, I realized that I had experienced transitions long before then.

I can remember what it felt like to not want for anything as a child. My parents owned a successful meat company, and they spared nothing when it came to me, the *only* girl. On Saturdays, I would get up and hit the streets with my mom. We loved to drive to Memphis, TN and shop. Memphis was only an hour and a half away from our home in Grenada, MS. My mother was my "momager" and I was her "Miss U.S.A." I toiled with a love/hate relationship of our shopping sprees. I loved to receive new things, but I hated trying everything on! I'm still this way. I want new clothes, but I don't want to try on anything—ever! This is perfectly normal, and I know you can relate. Anyway, pretty easy life, right? Being the only girl made life even easier because I had everyone wrapped around my finger, at least I thought I did. I was about seven years old when I started to notice my parents weren't as happy as they wanted my siblings and me to believe they were. They were godly people who took us to church almost every day. They, however, were so busy instilling religion in us that they missed the importance of being transparent with us. I believe this made the transition of their marriage to divorce even harder for my brothers and me. At only seven years old, I learned that failing to be honest with yourself prevents you from being honest with everyone else.

My father immensely struggled with honesty. As for my mom, she should have left. She had publicly (and privately) dealt with more than I ever could. She thought it was best we didn't know how unhappy she was until we had to know. As I mentioned before, I am my parents' only girl. Therefore, I spent many nights in their room. In fact, my bed was moved into their room for a little while. I often witnessed my father verbally and physically abuse my mom. I mastered sneaking out of the room in the middle of their quarreling to get one of my older brothers to protect my mom. My dad would say things like, "Oh, Daddy and Mama are just playing around," but we all knew better.

Soon, I noticed my dad would leave home for days at a time. I knew he would be gone for a while when I saw stacks of money on the table. This meant my mom would not have to worry about anything while he enjoyed the pleasures of his double life. As toxic as it may sound, I embraced it. We all did. It worked. He wasn't there, which meant that, along with provision still being made for us, there was peace at night.

Where there is unaddressed dysfunction,
brokenness becomes the norm.

I often missed him, and I paged his beeper only to receive a plethora of lies about his return (one-time for the people who know what pagers/beepers are). After learning what to expect from him, the lies no longer bothered me. I simply wanted to hear his voice because it reassured me that he was still alive. And although I had no desire to see my parents together, I still loved my father.

I experienced what I consider a whole-brokenness kind of childhood. As a child, I not only knew what transition was, but I knew all too well what it *felt* like. As the years progressed, I became very independent. I was no longer a spoiled brat. I did not get whatever I wanted, but I had everything I needed. As often as we went to church, church did not influence me to live for God. Don't get me wrong. Attending church taught me the best Sunday school lessons and gave us a village of people who were used by God in my father's absence. But experiencing God's goodness toward me is what compelled me to accept Jesus at only twelve years old. God strategically placed my mom where she needed to be to receive the provision He made when my father had completely walked away. As always, God was strategic, and He was intentional. We developed relationships with people who were essential to the speed of our breakthrough.

I should tell you that I am a musician, and I have been playing the piano since I was about three years old. My older brothers and a host of local musicians helped to cultivate my gift. I eventually shared my musical gifts at local churches and was compensated for my services. After my older brothers had married, moved away, and established their own families, this income assisted with the obligations of our household. My mom worked tirelessly, but meeting ends for her four remaining children, on a minimum wage income, proved extremely difficult for a single mother. We transitioned from what seemed to be Christmas all year to Christmas not coning until tax season, after Christmas had passed. We were delayed, but never denied. God kept us! He provided for us and positioned us to obtain more than I could have ever imagined.

People may read this short story of my childhood and say, "The struggle was real," but honestly, I cannot say God allowed us to struggle. In retrospect, I realize there were many families in our hometown who were worse off than us. They would have loved to experience a postponed Christmas gift opening, food stamps, and, for some children, a real mother's love. So, even in what I considered to be "struggling" as a child, I can see how our lack blessed so many others, as my mom was always serving, giving, and sharing. I am certain there were things we could have experienced that we did not because God honored the posture of my mother's heart. So instead of declaring that the struggle was real, instead, I say, the transition was real.

I have learned that transition can be ugly, but they are not designed to foster disaster, only development. Transition is God's way of staying ahead of us and making our crooked paths straight. When you experience transition, embrace it as an opportunity to experience God's preparation for the promise He's prepared for you. Allow me to share one of my most momentous transitions. I pray it helps you to understand that transitions will come, but they aren't meant to break you, only to make you into the person God has predestined you to be.

Transition One

I remember thinking that I was about to go off to college and live my best life. Although I was *not* far from home, I was not home! And boy did that excite me! I bought tons of new clothes so I could be prepared to stunt. I boasted, "I'm not worried about what people think about me," but I admittedly felt the need to impress people. I also struggled to admit that I did not have it all together. I was "built Ford tough" and being vulnerable just wasn't my thing. If I died, I would have just died. Ha!

Seriously though, I didn't choose to be this way. As I mentioned earlier, I was forced to become independent at only twelve years old. I was a child trying to figure out what bill needed to be paid and for what church I could play the piano to make sure my mom did not have to stress even more than she already did. We were left without many things when my father left, but I am glad to say we still had our home, dignity, and most of all, a saved mama.

I had THREE jobs in high school! While many people would celebrate my willingness to be independent and to push through, it, in fact, caused me to be very resentful. I had to be an adult and figure out adult things while my mind was still very immature. This experience caused me to feel like I did not have to accept constructive criticism from adults. I could take care of myself. Why would I listen to them? My mom had explained to me what college would be like and the emotions I would experience, but I did not listen. After all, she didn't even go to college. What did she know? I was as gullible as they came and truly convinced that I had this transition in the bag!

I will never forget the moment my mom had completely unpacked my dorm room and kissed me goodbye. I wept like a baby! All of those "I'm grown" statements of false security chased me all the way upstairs to my dorm room bed where I sat and cried the entire night. I distracted myself by setting out to kill my first look (outfit) for my freshman debut on campus. My sheltered soul determined that was a lie! Because I had been up most of the night sorting through all those emotions my mom warned me of, I overslept and ended up in hooping shorts and a t-shirt for my campus debut. I mean God really allowed me to experience the highest rank of humility during that first week of college!

This transition was the hardest thing I had ever done. I had officially left the familiar. I prayed more than I had ever prayed. I cried more than I had ever cried. I wanted to fit in and please God all at the same time. I wanted to be considered the "cool" church girl. And guess what else I wanted to do? I, the sweetest, kindest, and most loyal Trinity, wanted to date guys on campus even though I still dated my high school boyfriend. The pressure to do the right thing was on.

Transition tends to expose more about us as individuals than the new journey upon which we are actually embarking. I was a mess. The transition revealed me to me in a way I had never known. Choosing to diminish my mother's wisdom led to a turbulent transition. I thought I knew everything and did not know anything. ***As hard as it is for many of us to accept, Mama is almost always right.*** Sometimes we feel because people have not directly experienced what we are currently experiencing, they cannot advise us. This is not valid, true, or wise. ***Wisdom is not subject to a certain experience or certification, but it is received by those who are willing to adhere to the lessons of transition.*** Thanks be to God for people who have experienced transitions long before we have. They have the ability to see what we have yet to see. God uses them to speak to us.

There are two scriptures I want to leave with you concerning this matter:

" My son, do not let wisdom and understanding out of your sight, preserve sound judgment and discretion... "

(Proverbs 3:21 NIV)

" Those who trust in themselves are fools, but those who walk in wisdom are kept safe "

(Proverbs 28:26 NIV)

Seeking wisdom will add sound judgment to your thoughts and keep you from living a regretful life. Once I realized that much of what my mom said had validity, I embraced change, and I haven't been the same since. Wisdom, as well as transition, are necessary to become the person God has called you to be. It does not matter what transition you are experiencing now. Without wisdom, transition can quickly become a tragedy. With wisdom, transition can positively change the trajectory of your life.

What are you now declaring over your next transition?

Describe what real love is to you.

CHAPTER 2

Unfortunately, love has earned a bad rep because most of us have manipulated the terms of what love truly is. To understand what love is and how love should be given and received, you have to know from where love originates. You equally need to understand *Who* loved you first. You guessed it! It is God! God is love and love is God.

" Whoever does not love does not know God, because God is love "

(1 John 4:8 NIV)

As a young, adult female, the word love permeated through my text messages often. After watching my friends experience ongoing heartbreak, I prayed and asked God to keep me and give me discernment. I was also blessed to apply Scripture to help me understand what love looked and felt like. Only God, the creator and giver of love, can teach us what love truly is. If we are not careful, it is so easy to get caught up in a person's "love" for us without ever considering that they have done nothing to prove that their love for us is real. Yes, love should be proven and not only proven, but proven by sacrifice.

" For God so loved the world that he gave his one and only Son, that whoever believes in him shall not perish but have eternal life "

(John 3:16 NIV)

Real love provides the evidence of sacrifice. The book of John states, God gave. Friend, I have questions for which I do not just want responses, but also evaluation and reflection. What have you been giving? Is your giving sacrificial? Can you really say that you love how God loves? Are you loved by your family and friends with the love of God? God loved us so much that He gave His only son, Jesus, for us. That is a sacrifice only God would give for people who may never accept Him, or who merely acknowledge Him as "the universe." This love is unexplainable and underserved. You will never find anyone who will give up his or her only son to save your life. You just won't. I believe God wanted us to know how great His love for us is. He wanted us to know that love is sacrificial and unconditional.

We all love to discuss the five love languages and, for the most part, they are valid. However, we must know God's love language in order to love effectively. After some prayer, fasting, and research, I have discovered that God's love language is sacrificial giving. Isn't that beautiful? Now, I am in no way diminishing or discrediting the five love languages because I do believe they are legitimate assets necessary to give and receive love. But we must know that if those love languages are not expressed sacrificially, they are merely actions that do not effectively communicate love. As an adult of any age, it is imperative for you to be capable of identifying real love. Society has gotten so caught up in the five love languages, but God's love language must be implemented in order to make the other love languages identifiable, as well as, achievable. Coming into this knowledge reminds me of

Isaiah 55:8-9 (NIV), which reads,

" For my thoughts are not your thoughts, neither are your ways my ways,' declares the Lord. "

Friend, listen to me well. Don't get caught up in society's conditional terms of love. **I've learned that what is relevant isn't always righteous.** You should desire and strive for a *zoe* life, which, in Greek, means the God-kind-of-life. He is the creator of life, and He makes life good. Allow the thoughts of God to become your thoughts concerning love, and the rewards of sacrificial giving will be endless for you. Now that I've laid out that good receipt on authentic love, get into this next point.

One love language is *affection*. Affection is great, and many of us need it to know we are loved. It is me. I am us. I love for my husband to hug and kiss on me. Affection is definitely our thing, but if we showed each other affection only when things were good between us, would it really matter? The affection must become sacrificial in order for each of us to demonstrate love every single day. If Brandon leaving his shoes in the middle of the floor or me overreacting to a situation means affection will not be applied today, this love language becomes conditional. We know God's love is unwavering and unconditional. Therefore, affection and all the other languages must be shown when it is not so easy to freely give them. If love is a sacrifice, which we have biblically established, then authentic love must be sacrificially given.

Another love language I would like to discuss is *quality time*. We live in a generation where quality time is interpreted as "Netflix and Chill". Check this, if I have no job, nowhere to be, and nothing to do, is "Netflix and Chill" really quality time, or convenient time? I know this may not have been exactly what you wanted to hear, but I am not just a friend. I am an accountability partner. If you have mistaken convenience for quality time, it's okay. We are not here to judge. We are here to journey into a better version of ourselves. The fact that you have even picked up this book speaks volumes about your desire to not only do more, but to become more.

So, if you will, back to "Netflix and Chill" (I know I got bars). This idea of quality time being a love language has captured many of us in a quantity of conveniences. This is why it is important to know God's love language is sacrificial giving. Anyone not willing to make time for you, or anyone you are not willing to make time for, may be a situation of convenience, rather than love. This is often culturally referred to as a "situationship". A situationship is a relationship established out of convenience but bears no titles and serves no purpose between two people. Situationships often happen to those who cannot differentiate between sacrifice and convenience. Being able to identify quality time as a love language is not easy, especially when you have little experience with time that is genuinely quality. In this age of technology, where quality time involves everything except quality, it is easy to fall victim to convenience. When Brandon and I were courting, he often would sacrifice to give me the love language of quality time. He would often rearrange his schedule, leave a 12-to-16 hour work shift, and then drive an hour and a half to see me. It was not convenient. It required a sacrifice. It was equally a sacrifice for me to complete my Music Theory alone during the day, immediately following my classes, rather than with my peers at night so I could go on a date with him. I could go on and on with examples about the other love languages, but I think you get it. ***If it's not sacrificial, it is not love.***

1 John 3:1 (NIV) states,

" See what great love the Father has lavished on us, that we should be called children of God! And that is what we are! The reason the world does not know us is that it did not know him. "

The Bible says that God has lavished His love on us. According to the Webster's dictionary, lavish means to "expend or give in great amounts or without limit." Have you been receiving and giving love without limit? I know it is easy to only think of romantic love, but I would like to think all of us want to lavish love on not only our significant others, but on all people.

" Jesus replied, '"Love the Lord your God with all your heart and with all your soul and with all your mind. This is the first and greatest commandment. And the second is like it: Love your neighbor as yourself "

(Matthew 22:37-39)

My mom recently told me, "Your greatest blessing will come from loving people who don't love you." I thought her advice was so powerful. Loving people as we love ourselves requires us to have a real relationship with God. He is the first to know what it is like to give your best to people, and in return, they are—as the old adage goes—always a day late and a dollar short. Yet, He loves without limits on a daily basis. Of course, when we think about God, we think perfection, but perfection is not what God requires of us. He wants us to make progress. ***The good thing about God's grace is that it empowers us to do the things we are incapable of doing on our own.*** When we decide to love unconditionally, heaven builds a bridge of commerce where we can exchange our doubts for certainties, our fears for courage, and our brokenness for wholeness. That is what love does. Love is sacrifice that gives restoration and hope to every recipient. Grasping this concept will not only ignite your fire to love, but it will also enable you to love the way you are purposed to love.

Because I am a Christian woman, you would probably assume I have this love thing down pat. I wish I could say this is true, but if I could say that, I would not know God the way I do. As I mentioned earlier, to know love is to know God, and although many Christians have confessed that Jesus is Lord, many of us have not been intentional about building our relationship with Him. This is why we struggle to love without conditions. And if you are not yet a Christian, maybe someone who has not been intentional about his or her relationship with Jesus has misled you. Don't judge all of us by that one instance. We are all a work in progress. Since God created love and us, we are much more alike than you know.

Love is not something that develops overnight. Love is consistently maturing and being refined day in and day out. When I became intentional about my relationship with Jesus, I began to dissect what love genuinely is. I not only learned what my love could give to others, but I also learned what love could give me. ***Loving yourself is crucial to your success in relationships with others.*** Self-love can strengthen how you show love to other people. The more you love yourself, the less you require from people. Have you ever found yourself seeking your family and friends to fill voids in your life? For example, maybe you are not as happy as your friend, so you find yourself desiring to be around him more than normal because he fills your void of happiness. Or maybe you desire to be complimented when you change your hair or shoes because you struggle with insecurities. Yes, I get it. We all get it. If anyone tells you they don't, they may not be the most honest person. We have all dealt with insecurities and feelings of inadequacy that cause us to waver on loving ourselves. I have personally experienced this. Before I go any further, let me disclose and disclaim that I don't tell people my business, especially my marriage business, but I REALLY like you, so I'm making an exception.

Recently, Brandon and I were going back and forth about a list of my complaints about him. Yes, extra, most extra, and he literally gets to read about it! I have no problem admitting I'm a little crazy. Okay, a lot, but as our fabulous Aunt Tab says, "That's my business!" Anyway, we were going on and on. Well, I was. To know Brandon is to know he's very unbothered. I wish I was more like him in this area sometimes. My hubby isn't perfect, but when God created perfect, He sat Brandon Mitchell right next to perfect. Um hmm (turns on NeNe Leakes' voice) "I said what I said." Brandon's love for me radiates through his responses. I am presently shifting from laughing to crying tears of joy because it is so true. He has graciously taught me how to treat people you say you love, even when you do not like them in the moment. I know you are waiting for me to pour the tea in your cup. Haven't you heard that good things are worth waiting for? I have to work myself up to exposing my vulnerability. Vulnerability is something I am working on, and it is definitely working on me! Okay, I'm ready to let you in now, friends.

So, Brandon and I were having a major disagreement about something. I began to tell him everything he wasn't going to do. Ladies, you know how we do it. "First of all, what you not gon' do is . . .," and it went from there. In the middle of my rant, Brandon had a major outburst. Once again,

Brandon is very unbothered and chill. The fact that I had moved him to yell lets you know that I had gone too far. He yelled, "I'm NOT YOUR DAD!" In this moment, a weight so heavy fell on my heart. I realized that I had been holding my husband accountable for the voids and insecurities I had collected from fatherlessness. When I tell you that revelation hit different, it really hit different. I could not be mad anymore. Talking is not a struggle for me, but in that moment, I could not even talk. All I could do was sit and think. So many thoughts came to me as Brandon went on to explain what he meant. I heard him talking, but I continued to hear "I'm not your dad."

That was a God-moment for me. Instantly, I discovered something about myself I had never noticed. In my head, I contemplated, "So, I have a real daddy complex? It is true that Brandon has done none of these things for me to be telling him what he won't do. I saw my dad do this, not Brandon. OMG, I'm *that* girl." I felt dumb. I felt embarrassed. How could I expect him to love me out of my own thoughts that I had created against him because of my childhood experiences? I was making it hard to love me.

We all have those people that we love dearly, but because they struggle to love themselves, they feel you are obligated to love things about them that they do not even love about themselves! Whew, that was me. I had become that person and didn't know it until Brandon said what he said. It took a little time for me to process all of those thoughts and emotions. Finally, with prayer and therapy, I decided that I did not want to be hard to love. I had to figure out how to take out my own trash. I would no longer keep piling it up and blaming Brandon for the odor. That simply was not fair to him. I had to learn to love my good, bad, and ugly. Loving myself fully meant that I could acknowledge my past without allowing it to dictate my present or future. I decided I would no longer live in a space where I was limited to only certain levels of trust and love. Trust is a good thing. Love is a good thing, and all good things come from God. God gives us these good things without measure; therefore, we should also.

I no longer limit anything God does not measure. I allowed my insecurities to suggest my husband, the one who has been nothing but loving and faithful, was like my dad. When we choose to ignore the things that have hurt or traumatized us, we will subconsciously deflect our pain and hurt others. I get it. An ugly past is not always easy to address or acknowledge. But we must embrace the pain because what the enemy means for evil, God means for our good. My good friend, Fly Phyllis, says, "Pain makes us pray and prayer makes us powerful." When we allow God into those vulnerable places, His strength can be made perfect in our weaknesses (2 Corinthians 12:9 NKJV). Pain has a purpose, and it is not to hinder us, but to help us be more aware. You're probably wondering, "But how do I love myself out of pain so I can make it easier for people to love me and easier for me to reciprocate that love?" Turn with me to the book of 1 Corinthians, please. Ha! I love to have a word! I feel like if you are really my friend, then you know one thing about us is that we gon' laugh! Okay, we're about to read the Bible. Let's get serious even though I'm currently still chuckling myself. Let me give you a few scriptures that reminded me of how I should love myself. Here they are:

" Love is patient and kind;
love does not envy or boast;
it is not arrogant or rude.
It does not insist on its own way;
it is not irritable or resentful;
it does not rejoice at wrongdoing
but rejoices with the truth.
Love bears all things, believes all things,
hopes all things, endures all things.
Love never ends "
(1 Corinthians 13:4-8 ESV)

This passage of scripture defines what love is and how it should be demonstrated in the earth. It is vital for us to understand the very first part of this scripture. Loving yourself fully will require immeasurable patience and kindness. I thought I loved myself fully until I began to meditate on this scripture. If you don't know, I'm a fitness fanatic. I love living a healthy life. What I love most is the physical benefits. I mean I do love feeling good, but my physical appearance plays a significant role in how I feel. Call me vain, but I love loving how I look. I make no apologies for it because Jesus was fit. Yes, I went there. Don't even argue with me. Jesus ate fish and veggies, worked as a carpenter, and walked incessantly. How wasn't He fit? If we are striving to be like Jesus, then we should consider His physical lifestyle, too. Again, He walked everywhere. He ate balanced and nutritious meals. He also disciplined his body through fasting and prayer. I am certain Jesus had a six-pack... of abs that is! And I make an effort each and every day to be like my Savior. Okay, did I mention I tend to get sidetracked when fitness is mentioned? Keep me and my flesh in your prayers. Back to me thinking I fully loved myself—

I thought I fully loved myself until I began to mediate on 1 Corinthians 13:4-8. I had created a habit of always finding something wrong with myself. It did not matter how much I worked out, how perfectly I laid my edges, or how great my makeup looked. Something was always wrong. Brandon called me on it one day. He tends to "read" me often. I don't always like it, but his correction allows me to examine myself more. I realized that I experienced unnecessary anxiety from always wanting to be perfect, and we all know that is impossible. I somehow allowed social media to convince me that perfect is normal. What a lie! **The only thing we can do perfectly is be imperfect.**

1 Corinthians 13:4 tells us that love is *patient* and *kind*. I believe God was being strategic by having these two come first in the list of requirements for pursuing love. I am still learning to be patient and kind to myself. Honestly, the result is that I am starting to like myself more. I don't know about you, but all of that drama, anxiety, and frustration I brought on myself does not make me proud. It was just too much for me, and if it was too much for me, imagine what it was like for everyone else in relationship with me. ***It is unfair for us to expect people to tolerate, accept, and love things about us that we honestly don't like about ourselves.*** Not only are they unfair, but those feelings of entitlement also destroy relationships. If you allow yourself to be overwhelmed by nothing, what happens when something is really going on? I would literally crumble. Thank God, I eventually grew tired of lacking control. Extending grace and patience to myself has rewarded me more peace than I could have ever imagined. That peace enables me to follow through with love. When I am patient, I do not insist on my own way. When I am kind, I am less likely to be irritable and resentful. You see how this works?

I have learned to omit negative thoughts about myself and invite God's thoughts into my heart. Anytime I doubt, fear, project insecurity, etc., I can immediately change my mood when I proclaim, "This is not a God thought." God has given us power, love, and a sound mind (2 Timothy 1:7 NKJV). If my thoughts are not giving me power, love, and a sound mind, my thoughts are not from God. Since I have employed this strategy, I have developed an immense amount of patience and kindness for myself and others. ***Patience is the catalyst that makes it possible for us to love the way God has called us to love.*** What is more, I love that this passage of scripture starts with patience being not just one of the necessities of love, but the first necessity. Without first having patience, love is unachievable. Let me reiterate, God is intentional with all things, especially His Word. Practice being patient and kind, and you will find yourself loving what God loves and breaking away from the things that break His heart.

" Whoever gets sense loves his own soul;
he who keeps understanding will discover good "
(Proverbs 19:8 ESV)

This verse in Proverbs says to me, "Once we know better, we do and experience better." Thankfully, I have learned that love is sacrificial giving. Sacrificial giving means we have to sometimes love people who do not necessarily deserve our love. It took me a while to forgive my father for the things that transpired during my childhood. I swept most of it under the rug so I would not have to be vulnerable, but through love and love only did I receive my breakthrough. Once I forgave my father and chose to love him in spite of, the heavens opened for me. I have learned that anytime understanding takes place, better results follow; for understanding is the principle asset of wisdom. Proverbs 4:7 declares, "With all thy getting, get understanding" (KJV). And the New Living Translation of Proverbs 19:8 says, "To acquire wisdom is to love yourself; people who cherish understanding will prosper."

At the end of the first semester during my freshman year of college, I began to focus on Matthew 6:14-15, which admonishes, "If you forgive those who sin against you, your heavenly Father will forgive you. But if you refuse to forgive others, your Father will not forgive your sins." I was saved, but I was a practicing sinner. No one should be both! Therefore, I needed forgiveness. I stopped complaining about everything my dad did not and would not do. I gave it to God, and it was the best thing I could have ever done. God provided for me. He sent people to Mississippi Valley State University just for me. I struggled for almost the entire first semester of college, making only $125 per week, and using most of that for gas. I would also help my mom from time to time. Not to mention, I had a car note and car insurance that I could not afford, but I had to have a car. ONLY GOD. My roommate, Nicole, looked at me one day and said, "I'm going to pay your car note for you because you take me everywhere anyway." She still does not know how God placed her in that room just for me. A few weeks later, my friend, Demond, invited me to Cleveland, MS, to play alongside him during choir rehearsal. I thought we were just hanging out like always, but Demond was actually preparing to move and wanted to introduce me to his church family as his potential replacement. I had no idea. About one week later, he called and told me his plans and asked if I was interested in the job. Of course, I said yes. The rest is history. I started my new job at the church January of the following semester. God remained faithful to me and my mother. Not long after God blessed me with my new position, He blessed my mother with a promotion to a new and higher-paying position. She no longer needed me to help her. In fact, she began to help me. It was forgiveness, love, and sacrificial giving that brought this breakthrough into my life! I was so busy praising my pain, but when I gravitated toward praising the Lord and pursuing His healing, I became purposeful and prosperous. I want you to take some time and think now. How is your perspective of your current circumstances benefitting you? Are you really walking in love if you aren't forgiving?

"When we make a conscious effort to love and understand ourselves, we will inevitably discover good in others, and ourselves, even in dysfunctional relationships because love covers a multitude of sins"

(1 Peter 4:8)

" Three things will last forever- faith, hope, and love- and the greatest of these is love "

(1 Corinthians 13:13 NLT)

Moving forward, how can you receive love better?

How can you give love better?

What does a good friend look like to you?

CHAPTER 3

FRIENDSHIPS

Dear Friend,

The term friend has taken on a whole new meaning. I remember when we labeled people as friends after they had proven themselves to be worthy of that title. Now, we live in a world where friendship no longer requires fellowship, loyalty, or any sort of depth. In fact, most relationships are established through follows, DMs, and comments on social media. Some people have no clue how to socialize outside of the internet. Unfortunately, social media seems to have removed the value of genuine and meaningful friendships. As a result, this has caused many of us to lose the true meaning of friendship. For others, especially during a pandemic, it may take a lifetime to discover how friendship actually works. I am afraid that people will be convinced that social media is enough to build and sustain meaningful relationships. While it may appear easier to only have friends on social media, it is real-time relationship that cultivates the love about which we previously learned. I want to challenge you (if you haven't already) to place value on the friendships God has given you. If you struggle with trusting people, do not allow your experience with "frenemies" to deter you from the relationships God has strategically placed in your path. You will learn that you have no losses when you journey with God. All of your relationships will either be blessings or lessons. Everything literally works for your good. You will also discover that friends are like family members you get to choose! I believe in the power of divine assignments. We are assigned to help someone else. Some assignments are temporary, while others are permanent, or even occasional. But all assignments matter, as they give us reason to serve, commit, and love. Because God uses people, we need people.

" Two people are better off than one,
for they can help each other succeed.
If one person falls, the other can reach out and help.
But someone who falls alone is in real trouble.
Likewise, two people lying close together
can keep each other warm.
But how can one be warm alone?
A person standing alone can be attacked and defeated,
but two can stand back-to-back and conquer.
Three are even better, for a triple-braided cord
is not easily broken "

(Ecclesiastes 4:9-12 NLT)

I once heard someone say that life moves at the speed of your relationships. If you think about it, it is true. The place in life you are currently in is directly connected to the relationships you have. I often find myself thinking about how intentional God has been with the relationships He has blessed me to have. I previously thought friendships were overrated and, as a result, I failed to value people and my relationships with them. Growing up as the only girl of eight children, my brothers were my first friends. Because we fought so often, I cannot say we shared healthy friendships. Sibling rivalries are real, especially when you are the only girl and your mom's favorite (I really am her favorite even though she will never say it). Earlier in adulthood, it was challenging for me to maintain relationships with anyone outside of my brothers. Of course, growing up, I had friends from church and other functions, but I found maintaining relationships that my parents no longer hosted incredibly difficult.

For a long time, I thought it was other people with the problem, but I heard a sermon once during which a preacher stated, "If you find yourself having the same kind of problems with different people, then it is time for you to have a self-evaluation." This was an eye-opening moment for me. I had had many female friends tell me I had no filter. Some even described me as mean and said I had hurt their feelings at least once. Because I always had good intentions, I felt this notion was farfetched. I thought people just hated to hear the truth. At the end of the day, they had the problem, not me. I thought people needed to hear the truth, even if it hurt. In some cases, this is true, but I had to learn the hard way that truth and opinions are not one in the same.

We sometimes fail to realize that the way we think is shaped by our experiences. Having been a C.O.G.I.C. church kid and not exposed to much, I was judgmental. I was ignorant, too. I ignored that fact when judging others by my own truths. You may find this to be shocking about Your Friend Trin, but it is true. I have not always been the friend everybody wants or needs, and I certainly was not an advocate for reconciliation within relationships. Your Friend Trin, the girl who has flat-foot lied to impress people, is also the girl who loved holding on to receipts just in case I had a point to prove. Yes, that same girl had the audacity to be judgmental. Thanks be to God for His mercy and sufficient grace. I began to be transformed by the renewing of my mind around the age of twenty-five. I had learned something that I was not proud of. I had unconsciously made the traditions of religion the truth over the Word of God. Growing up in a Pentecostal church filled with self-righteous spirits, I had cultivated a nonchalant attitude toward the "truth," and my environment nourished this controversy. It did not matter how my words caused people to feel. I'd say, ***"The truth is the truth."***

It was after I hurt my dear friend when the Holy Spirit spoke to me and said,

"Just because it is the truth doesn't mean it is necessary to say."

This revelation sent a spiritual sword through my flesh. It broke me down. I started to notice God stripping me of my intangible discrepancies that kept me from becoming who He had called me to be. I started thinking before I spoke and asking myself if it was really necessary for me to share a particular thought. Boy, did this change my interactions with people. My conversations grew from being about people and their business to being more about business ventures, bettering myself, and building new relationships.

As I changed, my circle of friends gradually changed. The change brought about isolation for a while, but ***I have learned that isolation is often preparation for promotion.*** God needed to build my capacity for the caliber of friendships He would give me. I am amazed how learning to say only what is necessary will change your life. It changes who you are around and with whom you are able to connect. Thankfully, my level of productivity changed significantly as my circle of friends changed because who you are connected to has everything to do with how you produce. Once I began to experience this growth, I decided to never be bound to religion, tradition, or plain ignorance ever again. I started researching scriptures that I could meditate on that would help me become not only a better friend, but also a better Christian. Here are scenarios and scriptures that helped me transform my thinking and, consequently, my words:

" What goes into someone's mouth
does not defile them,
but what comes out of their mouth,
that is what defiles them "
(Matthew 15:11 NIV)

In the past, I loved exposing my enemies. I still struggle with looking beyond the faults of a flat-out liar, but I no longer desire to expose a liar because I have learned trying to expose someone else exposes more about me than

Scenario One

it does about them. It defiles me, which means it corrupts good character. People will perceive you to be messy, untrustworthy, and dishonorable when you set out to expose someone who has offended you. When you finish, what will it have proved? As a young adult who was adapting to different personalities in college, there were people I just did not like. It seemed that some people would lie simply because they had a tongue. I remember knocking my mom's bedroom door down on weekends to tell her what someone said about me. She would peacefully look at me and ask what I did to contribute to the problem, and when it was honestly nothing, she would quote Proverbs 12:19 (DBY) to me which states, "Truth lasts forever; lies are soon found out." Friend! One thing about God's Word is it does not lie, and it will never return void. I thought my mother was just being a saved mama until this scripture manifested in my life. It took a while, but I have learned to allow the Word of God to govern my life, especially my responses. When you know you have not done what people are saying you have done, let God speak for you. When we speak, our story will be heard, but when God speaks, all will be revealed.

" Those who guard their mouths and their tongues keep themselves from calamity "

(Proverbs 21:23 NIV)

We are not always are that we are participating in shady conversations. This is why we must be on guard. We will reap what we sow regardless of that

Scenario Two

seed being good or bad. And please believe, there is nothing worse than knowing you are reaping something bad as the consequence of putting your mouth on someone else. I get that shady conversations are just entertaining sometimes! We all know this; but ***participating in cheap conversation***

means you are giving calamity a warm welcome into your life. So even if you are around people who are discussing the shortcomings of others, don't be a contributor. This is a greater challenge when people are discussing someone of whom you are not particularly fond. Be aware that people will say things around you merely to see what your response will be. Believe it or not, there are certain people you are often around who don't like you. Be careful what you say and always pray for discernment. To make this simple, if you do not like getting messy, don't stir mess.

" The one who has knowledge uses words with restraint,
and whoever has understanding is even-tempered.
Even fools are thought wise if they keep silent,
and discerning if they hold their tongues "
(*Proverbs 17: 27-28 NIV*)

Scenario Three

If there is a right way, there is a wrong way, Friend. I don't know about you, but I prefer to have the kind of friends that I do not have to label as real. I do not have a group of friends and then a group of *real* friends. You are either my real friend, or you are not my friend. I foster these relationships by giving the same kind of loyalty, love, and respect I want to receive. Proverbs 17:27-28 is crucial to our success in maintaining healthy relationships because no two people are exactly alike. Because disagreement is inevitable, we must be able to respectfully disagree with our friends. I disdain for a relationship to be controlled by one person who has to have everyone see things his or her way only. Have you ever had a friend to lash out at you because your disposition opposed theirs? Maybe you have even been that friend. I know I have, and it caused me to rupture relationships that I needed. Through the ups and downs of friendship, one thing I have learned is I do not have to understand a person's decision to respect a person's decision. I have a short story to share that I believe will help those who are stubborn like me better digest this scenario.

I tend to be welcoming. I married at the age of twenty-three, and for a long time, Brandon and I did not have many married friends, at least not my age. He is four years older than me. Therefore, some of his friends were married, but I was the first one married in my circle of friends. Brandon and I were adamant about embracing our friends' significant others. We knew what it felt like to have our friends close the door on us when we got engaged. This, alone, deserves another book. Anyway, we were greatly intentional about not only bridging our personal friendships to our friendships as a couple by embracing our friends' fiancés and spouses. We felt that we should do this as friends. Typically, Brandon and I do not just call people friends. We are selective with who becomes our extended family because that is what friendships should be. To make this long story short, I chatted with Brandon's friends here and there. It was nothing specific or with reason, but I wanted to embrace them as our friends, not just Brandon's friends. This meant I had to make an effort to get to know them outside of him. Brandon did the same with my friends. Of course, we had our boundaries. I do not care how much of a friend you are, you are not sitting up and chatting with my man just because, and vice versa. As the popular social media meme says, "That's on Mary had a little lamb!"

Anyway, I later encountered a friend who did not subscribe to my way of acceptance. I had only spoken to her fiancé concerning his plans of proposing to her. After it had happened, and she had said, "Yes," I thought I had better take initiative to get to know him. This was important to me because I remember how some of my "friends" treated my husband, and I did not want to be that friend. I also remembered how it felt to have some of Brandon's "friends" completely disregard who I was to him. It encouraged me to never be that kind of friend when my friends got married, accepted a new job, or experienced promotion in their lives. This was truly my only reason for attempting to embrace my friend's fiancé as both my and Brandon's friend. We did not converse much at all. I may have texted him here or there about a basketball game or played iMessage games (because I'm kind of addicted to those, and I love to emasculate my male friends on those games, ha!).

Later, my friend and I were conversing when I mentioned something about a previous conversation with her fiancé. She bluntly told me she did not want me talking to him. Because of our bond, and me clearly not having a problem with her talking to Brandon, I was offended. She knew my character well enough to know that I would never disrespect her or her relationship, but that did not alter her request. I was blown away. Her request did not necessarily bother me, but I struggled to understand it. Don't all of us want our friends to know our significant others at some point? Of course, not like we do, but don't we want them to act like our significant others exist, especially after an engagement? I could not understand why she would request this. Without question, I gave her a piece of my mind. At the time, I was not mature enough to not understand her decision and still respect it. I said, "The fact that you even requested this, I am deleting your future husband's number, and I will never contact him again, not even if you are with me and short of breath will I use his number." I know, I know. I told you, God has done a great work in me!

Per usual, it took a few days, but the Holy Spirit revealed to me that I was wrong to expect my normal to also be my friend's normal. Every marriage is different because people are different. I think the lesson of this story is evident, but for those who may not have gotten it, we do not have to understand a person's decision to respect it. When I later texted my apology to her, that is exactly what the Holy Spirit led me to say. Our relationship has continued to grow and flourish. Her not wanting me to build a relationship with her husband the way I had with my other friends' husbands had nothing to do with me and everything to do with how she wanted to conduct her marriage, and guess what? That was her business! It was not for me to understand. I believe yielding to her request both strengthened our bond and placed a stamp of longevity on our friendship. Be intentional about becoming the friend who does not have to understand your friend's decision but will still respect your friend's decision.

We find offense in things we should not. The only person who has to live with decisions is the person making them. Before you find offense in their decision, ask yourself how that decision actually affects you. You will find yourself living peacefully and strife-free. What you will discover is the best part about a friendship is no two people are the same. That is what makes friendship enjoyable and beneficial.

The Power of The Apology in Friendship

Apology - a written or spoken expression of one's regret, remorse, or sorrow for having insulted, failed, injured, or wronged another.

" Therefore, confess your sins to each other
and pray for each other so that you may be healed.
The prayer of a righteous person is
powerful and effective "
(James 5:16 NIV)

A person who does not apologize should not be labeled as a friend. If a person cannot acknowledge their own mistakes with others, they do not value people or relationships. It is no secret that we live in a very prideful world where people find it embarrassing and unacceptable to be wrong. Everyone wants to be right. Most of us would rather right our wrongs by being nice to people rather than addressing our mistakes and taking responsibility for our actions. Because of this, our personal growth and our relationships have been stifled. When we cannot acknowledge that we feel regretful, we cannot access the gift of repentance. Further, when we refuse to repent, we often forfeit the grace of being forgiven by others, but most importantly, by God. Taking accountability for our actions grants us restoration and redemption.

Most people think apologizing is admitting to being wrong, but apologizing says we regret not only making a mistake, but the consequences caused by our mistake Made plain, apologizing says, you care more about how your decision has affected the person you have offended rather than what your intentions were. Sometimes, we have good intentions, but they are frequently met with poor skills or execution. And true enough, some people deserve a good old-fashioned clap back from time to time, but controlling our own responses is the first step to a strife-free life.

I have a few questions. Why is it easier to apologize only when we feel we are wrong? Why is it easier to apologize to everyone but us? Our relationship with ourselves is pivotal in how we conduct ourselves in relationships with others. The greatest war we will ever fight is the war against our own flesh. This is why we need the Holy Spirit to direct, correct, and protect us because we are tempted in every way to succumb to our flesh. In Romans 7:18 (NLT), Paul declares, "And I know that nothing good lives in me, that is, in my sinful nature. I want to do what is right, but I can't." Let me tell you this. When I say I can relate, I can! I have found myself feeling like Paul in so many instances. My heart wanted to do the right thing and apologize, but my mind asserted, "She shouldn't have tried me." I know somebody felt that. There are some people who have the ability to take us to the deepest depths of our flesh, but that is not really the issue.

The real issue is us feeling like God needs our help in handing vengeance. He does not. ***In fact, if we really wanted to help God, especially as believers, we should practice being a reflection of Him.*** Every day, God gives us new mercies. He extends grace, which enables us to do things we are incapable of doing in our strength. My friend, if we truly desire to see God's face, we have to tap into His sufficient grace (more bars). Seriously, though! Paul was sharing a moment of transparency that all of us can say we have experienced. He found himself in constant war with his flesh. It was not until later in 2 Corinthians 12:9 (NLT) that Paul heard God say, "My grace is all you need. My power works best in weakness." Paul goes on to say, "So now I am glad to boast about my weakness, that the power of Christ can work through me." If you know anything about Paul, you know He was not always Paul. He was Saul, a sinner. You see how that works? Saul, the sinner, turned into Paul with the power. I can hear my friend, Vicky, screaming, "That's good!" And that certainly is good news.

God's grace gives us the power to exchange our weaknesses for His strength, and rather than remaining where we are, grace empowers us to become who God has called us to be. Paul is a testament to how God's power must first work in you before He is able to work through you. When we fail to acknowledge our wrong, we sacrifice the experience of His strength being made perfect in our weakness. Regret knocks at the door of every person who chooses to be prideful and unaccountable. Unfortunately, there are people who will never meet their full potential in God because the idea of being accountable scares them. When brokenness is all a person knows, breaking away from it can be terrifying because being whole is unknown territory.

This is why people find apologizing to be challenging; it causes us to face our fears. When we face our fears, we have to be vulnerable. When we are vulnerable, we have to be humble. When we are humble, we experience God's sufficient grace. The problem is we want grace without humility or vulnerability. A genuine apology requires a humble heart and the ability to be vulnerable. In order for us to experience the power of accountability, we must be willing to step into both humility and vulnerability. Now I know you may be thinking this is strictly about giving an apology, but this also about being able to receive an apology.

Unforgiveness floats on the wings of a prideful and entitled spirit. The truth is nobody owes us anything, not even an apology. The sooner we accept this, the less complicated our lives will be. We must be able to receive apologies from people who have yet to learn what it means to foster relationships that are conducive to God's word. ***Our success is solely predicated on our ability to extend grace to others.*** Unfortunately, every person who confesses the prayer of salvation will not learn this lesson. This is why we must be diligent to cultivate an environment where weaknesses are a good thing because God's strength is made perfect in weakness. The grace of God makes repentance possible. It also makes the ability to be accountable rewarding, but the power of the apology is only as powerful as the change that follows it.

On the whole, some friendships will only be temporary. Some friendships will be permanent. Some friendships will grow. Other friendships will be the beginning of lifelong partnerships. But your character will determine how effective those relationships are in your life. Good character will yield meaningful relationships. Being able to acknowledge when you are wrong will give your relationships longevity. Last, but not least, accepting that you are not assigned to everyone and that you cannot convince people to place value on the relationship they have with you is key to quality and pleasurable friendships.

I pray that you will become the friend who is willing to build, give, and forgive

How would you rate yourself on a scale of 1-10 as a friend?

What can you do better in your friendships to increase your ranking?

What does financial freedom look like to you?

CHAPTER 4

FINANCIAL FREEDOM

Money and I have definitely had our share of ups and downs. I was not fortunate enough to have a college fund or inheritance when I graduated high school and college. Therefore, my twenties were all about the grind. I do not specialize in being spoiled or entitled like most people in my generation. Instead, I specialize in survival. For a while, survival was all I knew. Let's be clear. Nothing is wrong with being built to survive, until survival is all that you know. ***A person with a survival mentality must be willing to adopt a prosperity mentality if he/she wants to end surviving and enter into prosperity.*** I am not ashamed to admit that it took nearly most of my twenties to realize I had nourished my survival mentality and starved my potential.

If it were not for my Pastors, Sino & Kellie Agueze's teachings, I likely would not have pursued writing this book or considered any other business opportunities. Through the divine teachings of my pastors, I recognized I was living under a financial curse. I wanted to be rich, but along the way, I settled for being well-off. I additionally settled to pay my bills and have some left over for a few trips during the year. That was a better life than I had growing up, so I was satisfied with it. Sadly, I procrastinated executing any business idea that God would give me. I even procrastinated finishing the production of songs I knew had major potential. With no doubt, God had given me gifts that would empower me to break the curse of poverty, but I was subjecting myself to the curse by not doing what God had given me to do.

At times, we do not understand how not fully executing the vision God has given us holds us back. Many of us find ourselves stagnant and broke because we never trust God or the vision God has given us. Yes, ***you can trust God, yet fail to trust that He has given you everything you need to be financially free.*** I'm using the word, "free" because growing up I heard a lot of people say they wanted to be financially secure and I, unfortunately, adopted that mindset. I never heard anyone say they wanted to be financially free. Obviously, secure and free are not one in the same. ***An "enough" mentality produces an "enough" reality.*** The Bible says, "So a man thinketh, so is he," This is why we have to gain clarity on these two words. When I hear the word, "freedom," I immediately think, no boundaries, which means more than enough or freedom to do whatever you desire. When I hear the word secure, I think safe. In other words, you can get your bills paid, but you may not necessarily experience abundance. What about you? Let's break these two words down so we fully understand what we are giving life to when we speak about money. Sorry, I'm not sorry. It is the former educator in me.

Secure

free from risk of loss

Free

not obstructed, restricted, or impeded

As I stated, secure, simply summed up, is playing it safe. A person who is striving to be financially secure may never pursue entrepreneurship, invest in one of his or her talents, or invest in anyone else's vision. On the opposite side, a person who is in pursuit of financial freedom models it through limitless pursuit. These people will invest in themselves because they understand that their success is dependent upon their presentation and quality. These people will also invest in others because they understand the law of reciprocity. Let's declare this together, "I want financial freedom, not financial security." If you settle for financial security, you cannot obtain financial freedom, but with financial freedom, you will have security limitlessly.

Like generations before, many of us have passed up several opportunities and procrastinated ourselves into a life of complacency. We have suppressed the thoughts that can lead us into a life of overflow and found ourselves satisfied with having enough. I definitely had. Before my mind was transformed, I subconsciously settled for a life I never desired. I loved teaching, but I knew there was more for me to do. I always felt I should do full-time ministry and become a successful songwriter and author. However, my monthly check was consistent, and I knew I had health insurance. I was "adulting". I resolved that my dreams would someday come to fruition. Well, ***someday goals are just as good having no goals***.

Fortunately, we serve a God who is faithful enough to meet us right where are. He not only used the field of education to prepare me, but He also used it to strengthen the skills I would need for the next season of my life. For years, I thought to myself, "Am I really supposed to do this for thirty years, retire, and die?" And I am not saying that teaching equals a bad life because teachers are much more than teachers. We are, in fact, parental figures, nurses, counselors, and most of all, friends in the classroom. I loved playing these roles, but I did not love the job. I loved the students, but not the duties. I knew the desires God placed in my heart, even as a young child, and those desires could not be fulfilled with the salary I was receiving.

It took a while for me to grasp this, but I learned, through utilizing my gifts, that I could do much more than play the roles. I could provide opportunities for others. By utilizing my gifts, I could become the answer to someone else's prayer and provide relief for underpaid educators and low-income families throughout the world. I was in prayer one morning when the Holy Spirit spoke these words to me: ***"If you only have enough, you are not doing enough."*** We serve a God who does exceedingly, abundantly, and above all we could ask or think. He says in His Word that He has made us in His likeness and in His image. We should also live in God's supernatural overflow and abundance. After all, it is a fact that God's word does not return void; we simply do not apply it to our lives. What I have found to be the greatest barrier in the application process is that we fail to see what God sees. We trust Him, but not His will for our lives; and His will, my friend, should be your reality. It is certainly above all you could ask or think.

Without question, God is a good God, but do you know what makes Him better than good? The fact that He still cultivates and refines our gifts when we choose to misuse, belittle, and discount them. Even when you do not realize it, God is molding and shaping you. God is nurturing gifts you have yet to discover. Things you have yet to see are being manifested. If I were you, I would make it personal and prophesy those last two sentences over myself. And when you finish, write this scripture down and start memorizing it.

" But as it is written, 'Eye has not seen, nor ear heard, nor has it entered into the heart of man the things which

God has prepared for those who love Him "

(1 Corinthians 2:9 NKJV)

I know you may be in a place of uncertainty right now, but don't worry because God is certain. It is apparent that He is calling you to more, but your circumstances have caused you to become complacent. Perhaps what you are doing is not fulfilling, but it affords you the ability to pay your bills and live comfortably. Maybe you want financial freedom, but your employer does not exactly share the wealth. And maybe you deserve the promotion, but your efforts have been overlooked. It even appears that time has passed you by and you're saying, "I'm almost ___ years old. I need to just figure something out because it is too late for me to do what God gave me to do." I get it. We all get it! I want to remind you that God is eternal, which means He exists outside of time. Therefore, He has the power to redeem our time. It may seem that I am going off the topic of financial freedom, but it is really important for you to understand how trivial our time is compared to God's timing. According to Philippians 4:19 (ESV), He will supply our needs according to His riches in glory and in His perfect timing. ***That is good news. God does not need our situation to be right to move on our behalf. God does not need our credit score to approve us, and He certainly does not require our timeline to be on time.*** In fact, the reason He is always on time is because He cannot be late. God is eternal.

Jeremiah 29:11 (NIV) states,

" For I know the plans I have for you, " declares the Lord, " plans to prosper you and not to harm you, plans to give you hope and a future. "

The Good News Bible translation says,

" I alone know the plans I have for you,
plans to bring you prosperity and not disaster,
plans to bring about the future you hope for. "

So, financial freedom is not only our desire, it is God's desire for us. I am beginning to feel overwhelmed with emotion as I write because I know God wants us to see that He is the one who places our greatest desires within our hearts. The future we hope for is often God foreshadowing His plan, and ultimately His promise. Do you really think your awesome business ideas, knack to go above and beyond just because you are a "perfectionist," and level of creativity are attributable to you? No, these attributes are a preview of what God wants to do for and through you. Don't sleep on yourself because 1 John 4:4 (NASB) declares, "You are from God, little children, and have overcome them; because greater is He who is in you than he who is in the world."

Think of it this way—when you experience ideas, visions, and opportunities that seem to be unreal, undeserved, and far out of your reach, it is the greatness within you rising up and coming into alignment with your purpose. Sometimes, you are fearful because you do not understand exactly what is happening. The fear of the unknown can be terrifying, but if you think about it, our "after" often is greater than our before. We do not have to stress, worry, or fear because God never gives vision without provision. ***God has already provided the people assigned to help you carry out the vision and the finances and strength for you to execute.*** Decide that you will have all that God has planned for you to have. God has called all of His children to prosper. There will be times when we do not understand the plan, but we must be willing to trust it anyhow because the fact remains that His thoughts are not our thoughts, and neither His ways our ways (Isaiah 55:8-9 NIV). As the young people say, I'm about to "reach". If prosperity, abundance, and overflow are God's desire for me, settling for "enough" is a sin.

James 4:17 (NKJV) declares,

" Therefore, to him who knows to do good and does not do it, to him it is sin. "

As Pastor Sino says, "Don't look at me; look at the Bible!" If God's plans are to prosper me and to give me the future I hope for, why would I continue shortchanging that? Today, we get out of our own way (but did you catch that bar though? Ha.). I was recently conversing with my friend, and we were discussing Galatians 6:9 (KJV), which says, "And let us not be weary in well doing: for in due season we shall reap, if we faint not." My question to her was, who determines when it is our due season? Does God determine this or do I determine it? Our faith, obedience, and persistence move the heart of God. Therefore, yes. ***We determine our due seasons, for our due seasons are predicated on our ability to work while we wait. I*** know, I know. Some of you scholars are feeling a type of way and tempted to close my book. But listen, the woman with the issue of blood was DETERMINED. Jesus was not on a His way to heal her. He was headed to someone else's house! Her faith and perseverance shifted a twelve year wait into a DUE season. ***She received her healing because she decided to be a different kind of desperate.***

How many of us can say we are desperate for God to deliver us from things such as insecurities, pride, and bad character that hinder us from accessing the God-kind of life in which miracles can be our norm? Her desperation moved the heart of Jesus so much that, in a crowd of thousands of people, He knew someone desperate for deliverance touched him. Peter even said,

"Master, there are so many people on each side of you. Anyone could have touched you." In Luke 8:46, Jesus says, "Someone touched me; I know that power has gone out from me."

Friend, I want to ask you a question, and I really want you to think about it before you respond. Is the fervor of your pursuit causing the power of God to be released over your life? If the woman with the issue of blood had resolved that twelve years of suffering meant she was destined to live that life, she would not have received her healing. If this woman were concerned with the naysayers in the crowd whispering, "That is that woman with the issue of blood," she would not have pressed through thousands of people. She was embarrassed, afraid, ***yet she was determined to go from begging to believing.*** She determined her due time and refused to let her current circumstance dictate the rest of her life.

You also have a greater power within you to determine your due season. If you truly desire to see God step out of His eternity and move into your time, you have to work your faith. ***Most of us have declared, "I got next," because we are not moving now. But next will always be your portion if now continues to be optional.*** When we see others flourishing, we should take notice that the work did not start when they began to flourish. Long before then, they had been working their faith, and flourishing is the result of that work. Just like the woman with the issue of blood, your pursuit of, perseverance toward, and desperation for deliverance can shift you from next to now. Everyone will not experience financial freedom because everyone will not pursue the power it takes to have it. ***I have made a decision to pursue the power.*** When Jesus is sitting at the right hand of the throne interceding for me, I want Him to stop and tell God, "Trinity just touched me." That is the kind of faith with which I want to pray. That is the kind of faith that moves God.

The more desperate we are, the more due we are for God's power and prosperity to find us. The time is NOW, not NEXT.

" For we are God's handiwork,
created in Christ Jesus to do good works,
which God prepared in advance for us to do "
(Epheisans 2:10 NIV).

"What can you do now to set yourself up for financial freedom?

In What area of your life do you need more accountability?

CHAPTER 5

We all have heard the speech about accountability. Most of us have used it to reprimand friends, children, family members, and even coworkers. You know, it goes a little like this, "Take responsibility for your actions. Do unto others, as you would have them to do unto you. Apologize when you are wrong." Because of these statements and approaches, the word "accountability" has gained a negative connotation. Many of us have only heard or used this word during conflict. But I believe it is most necessary when there is no conflict. If we encouraged and applied accountability more when conflict was not our point of interest, we would have fewer interactions that revolve around conflict.

Unfortunately, accountable is an adjective and attribute few possess and a characteristic often missing in people's overall character. Why? Although we have heard and used this word time and time again, I believe that most of us do not know what it actually means. There is a perception of what it means, but who actually stops to define words like *accountability?* Me. I do. It's the accountability for me because what you cannot define, you cannot demonstrate. Rather than embracing the general concept of what accountability means, I wanted to dive deeper. When I did, I not only raised the standard for myself, but for everyone connected to me. Being accountable is an attribute that anyone in a relationship with me must possess. In fact, there should be a "must have" list for every relationship, and accountability should be at the top of it. I will elaborate shortly, but first, here's the definition:

Accountable

subject to the obligation to report, explain, or justify something; responsible, answerable

Now that we know what it means to be accountable, do you ever find yourself struggling to be obligated? Obligations truly challenge me. I like to do what I want to do and when I want to do it. However, when I have obligations (even to things I like to do), I find myself procrastinating. Can you relate? The constant struggle between obligation and procrastination is what often holds our dreams and visions captive.

Captivity

the condition of being imprisoned or confined

Procrastination

the action of delaying or postponing something

When we fail to commit to our obligations, we instead commit to procrastination, which leads us into a life of captivity. For example, you end up working a job for years and wondering where you would be if you had only committed those two to three hours per day toward developing your own business plan. Or you find yourself in a relationship that is not fulfilling or purposeful, but you have been in it so long that you think, "I may as well stay." This is why the ability to execute is a crucial part of being accountable. ***Doing what you know to do is much easier said than done, but making the decision to execute your vision really does determine your destiny.***

I recently wrote in my journal, "Learn to take ownership of your obligations, or your obligations will take ownership of you." Rather than living a life where things chase you down, execute a plan that enables you to be proactive and avoid the unnecessary debacles life can present. For example, being proactive can prevent student loan offices from calling your job to garnish your paychecks when all you had to do was call and make payment arrangements, a previous relationship that should have been severed surfacing and causing problems after you have met your soul mate, or even worse, having a car accident that totals your car due to bad tires when you could have simply made an appointment to have your tires replaced. I am learning to take ownership of my obligations so that my obligations don't continue to have ownership of me. ***Life is happening now, not next.***

Discipline yourself to handle things in the *now* because the *next* is often too late, and not promised to you!

My friend, Jason Gibson, has a clothing brand named "Pray, Plan, & Execute." I could not have thought of a mandate so simply stated, yet so vital to living a life of accountability. The good thing about this trio is wherever they exist, so does accountability. Praying, planning, and executing are not only sensible, but biblical.

PRAY

" Do not be anxious about anything, but in everything by prayer and supplication with thanksgiving let your requests be made known to God. And the peace of God, which surpasses all understanding, will guard your hearts and your minds in Christ Jesus "

(Philippians 4:6-7 ESV)

PLAN

" Commit your work to the LORD, and your plans will be established "

(Proverbs 16:3 ESV)

EXECUTE

" Just as the body is dead without breath, so also faith is dead without good works "

(James 2:26 NLT)

We do not naturally possess accountability. You have to sow into being accountable. You plant the seeds of praying, planning, and executing and, thereby, reap accountability. I hate to discuss three things: "couldas, wouldas, and shouldas." When I tell you I do not have time for it, I do NOT! I'm laughing here, but seriously! I believe we have the power to create our own realities. When we reflect on what we could have, would have, and should have been, it becomes very evident that we failed to pray, plan, and execute. Implementing these three streams of accountability will not lead you into failure but into a life of unwavering faith. Let's reflect on the scriptures I gave you. In Philippians, we are reminded to trust God's timing by not being anxious for anything. When we do this, He will reward us with peace that surpasses all understanding! In Proverbs, we learn that if we commit our works unto the Lord, our plans will be *established*.

Yep, we have a new vocabulary word.

Establish

to introduce and cause to grow and multiply

I am getting excited, okay! I am reassured that if I surrender myself and my vision to the will of the Lord, He will reward me with peace that surpasses my understanding and cause my vision to grow and multiply! I heard the Lord say, "The well will never run dry when it has been established by the Living Water himself." My prayer is that you will allow God to establish you. We do not have to live believing "nothing good lasts forever" because God's word completely opposes that perspective. We do not live by the world's words, but by God's Word.

" The Lord will guide you continually, giving you water when you are dry and restoring your strength.
You will be like a well-watered garden,
like an even flowing spring "
(Isaiah 58:11 NLT)

" And I will always guide you and satisfy you with good things. I will keep you strong and well.
You will be like a garden that has plenty of water,
like a spring of water that never goes dry "
(Isaiah 58:11 GNT)

" And the Lord shall guide thee continually,
and satisfy thy soul in drought,
and make fat thy bones:
and thou shalt be like a watered garden,
and like a spring of water,
whose waters fail not "
(Isaiah 58:11 KJV)

Accountability leads to supernatural abundance. A failure to be accountable results in stagnancy.

Stagnancy

characterized by lack of development, advancement, or progressive movement.

A life that does not have purpose does not exist. Your faith is the tool that activates the work ethic to accomplish and manifest what you see by faith. If you are not working on what you envision, my question to you is, do you really believe in your vision? The level of your results is a direct indication of your belief. Please stop and read that again, friend. Have you been getting minimum results because you put in minimal effort? Oftentimes, we fail to be accountable because of fear of the unknown. In many cases, we receive vision and immediately think about what we do not have.

The enemy's plan is to keep us from executing the strategies necessary to receive our breakthrough. I have become intentional about reminding the enemy of God's Word when he reminds me of my inadequacies. We have to stop analyzing what we have to make it happen and instead trust that if God gave the vision to us, we already have what and who we need to make it happen! When you are certain God has given you a vision, you must pray, plan, and execute. Everybody loves to quote Ephesians 3:20, but few realize that God gives us an obligation in it. God can do exceedingly, abundantly, and above all we can ask or think – ACCORDING TO THE POWER THAT WORKS WITHIN US! We have a role to play to obtain the life of infinite abundance God has called us to. What is truly working in you? Is it power or excuses? Do your little results match your little belief? God did not give us excuses, but He did give us power. I will show you.

" For God hath not given us the spirit of fear;
but of power, and of love, and of a sound mind "
(2 Timothy 1:7 KJV)

This discussion about accountability may become uncomfortable, but it is because I love you. You have learned that I take pride in being a good friend. Good friends tell friends what they need to hear even if they do not want to hear it. So, here it is! ***God has given you everything you need to move NOW, not next. Yesteryear's faith does not belong in your NOW***. Talking about what you are going to do next is only okay if you are taking advantage of what God is doing NOW. We have rested in excuses instead of our power long enough. Friend, you are not waiting on God. He is waiting on you! God is always moving, but in order for us to collide with Him in faith, we have to move, too! We can never expect to experience a supernatural move if we are sitting still in the natural. ***If you cannot do what is necessary in the natural, there is no point in expecting the supernatural to be your portion.*** What is more, we must understand that we are made in the image of our Creator. Therefore, we are all creatives! God gives us vision, but it is up to us to make His will our reality. You are the rightful owner of power, love, and a sound mind. Fear, doubt, and hopelessness do not belong to you, so stop taking ownership of the things that keep you from creating a new reality. If you are feeling any emotions that do not reflect what you have been given by God, rebuke them! Emotions were never meant to control, but to make us aware of ourselves and of God's presence. When emotions are misplaced, poor decision-making is typically the result. Say it with me. "I have power, love, and a sound mind." Friend, listen to me and listen to me well. Don't just confess that it is your turn before you actually decide to take your turn. It is only your turn if you take it. I love how the writer puts it in the following scripture:

" I have observed something else under the sun.
The fastest runner doesn't always win the race,
and the strongest warrior doesn't always win the battle.
The wise sometimes go hungry, and the skillful
are not necessarily wealthy. And those who are
educated don't always lead successful lives.
It is all decided by chance, by being in the
right place at the right time "

(Ecclesiastes 9:11 NLT)

If you consistently fail to be accountable, it is impossible to have the chance to be in the right place at the right time. ***The time to be accountable is now.***

NOW (adverb)

at the present time or moment; without further delay; immediately;
under the present or existing circumstances, as matters stand.

During the breakout of the COVID-19 pandemic, I have learned how important it is to be ready! If you stay ready, you don't have to get ready. Personally, this is the most essential component of being accountable—staying one step ahead. I had to change my prayer from "God position me," to "God help me to adjust my posture in the position you have already placed me." This prayer changed my life instantly! I mean, I was steadfast and unmovable in that "God position me" prayer. Then one day, the Holy Spirit brought this repetitious prayer to a halt. He invasively whispered, "Why are you so convinced that you need a certain position to receive a certain blessing? If you have the right posture of prayer, you already have the position." That's when Matthew 6:33 (KJV) came alive for me!

" But seek ye first the kingdom of God, and his righteousness; and all these things shall be added unto you. "

Suddenly, my approach to prayer changed and the visions God had given me became the vision for *NOW, not next.*

I urge you that the time is now. Do whatever you need to do to see God's will for your life become your reality. If that means quitting the job, do it. If that means moving, do it. If that means ending certain relationships that cause you to feel like chasing God's dream is too much, do it! God has plans to give us the future for which we hope. He has plans for us to prosper, not to bring disaster upon us. God wants to give us a rich and satisfying life—a life where exceeded expectations and miracles are normal. But that life is only available to the believer who chooses to be *accountable*. ***If you are willing bear the reward, you must be willing to bear the responsibility. Your reward, your responsibility.***

In what way do you think a healthy acceptance of accountability will enhance your life?

In what ways do you show appreciation?

Take a moment to evaluate yourself before answering this question.

CHAPTER 6

Appreciate

1. recognize the full worth of.

2. understand (a situation) fully; recognize the full implications of

APPRECIATION is another word that is often articulated but poorly demonstrated. Honestly, I have had my share of lessons in this area. It is one thing to appreciate people for what they can do for you and another to appreciate people for who they are, despite whether they are able to do things for you. Learning the difference helped me to cultivate the skills necessary to maintain healthy relationships outside of small favors and invitations. I have learned to accept people for who they are and love them where they are. Treating people better will make your life better. This is a concept I value above all else. Appreciation to some people is the act of reciprocity. To me, appreciation is realizing someone's worth to God first, and treating him or her accordingly. As believers, we should value what and who God values, even if we feel a person does not deserve it. Our feelings do not change the value God places on others. To see God's love manifested in every aspect of our lives, we must begin to value His people in the way He's called us.

" Love one another with brotherly affection.
Outdo one another in showing honor "
(Romans 12:10 ESV)

" This is my commandment,
that you love one another as I have loved you "
(John 15:12 ESV)

Y'all, I ain't gon' lie. This scripture made my heart race. Like, hold on God. Wait. This is one to process because this means we have to love people who do not love us, people who are simply haters, and people who plot to destroy us. God exhorts us to love *all* people with brotherly affection and outdo one another in showing honor! Whew, chile! Practicing this scripture is easy with people we feel reciprocate our love, but it is extremely difficult with people who are not so easy to love.

" Do not forget to show hospitality to strangers,
for by so doing some people have shown
hospitality to angels without knowing it "
(Hebrews 13:2 NIV)

Showing honor and appreciation should be our greatest pursuit each and every day. Since becoming an adult, I have learned it is easy to treat people how you feel they should be treated based on your own experience in their position. For example, let's say you have never experienced healthy relationships, so you feel the person you are in a relationship with does not deserve to be trusted. Although you know it is wrong to be controlling, manipulative, and even deceptive, you employ these characteristics to ensure you are not betrayed. Another example is treating "outside" people rudely with the excuse of, "This is just the way the world goes." Who are outside people? Let me help you.

1. Your in-laws
2. Your supervisor
3. The mother/father of your child
4. Your stepchild, stepmom, or stepfather

Now, I know this is possibly making you uncomfortable, but it's okay. Uncomfortable conversations are necessary and pivotal to our success as friends, coworkers, co-parents, and family members. Here's to another moment of transparency!

"What we don't appreciate, depreciates."

– Sino Agueze

Early in college, I decided I no longer wanted to have a relationship with my father. I was completely over being disappointed. Sadly, I began to highlight every mistake he had ever made. This helped to validate my decision, and although my reasons were pretty valid, my response was not. I failed to realize how blessed I was to have my dad (even though I knew he could have been a better father). He was far from the best dad but also far from the worst dad. Thanks to Brandon, I was able to forgive my father, and I learned to honor him.

Because of my choice to honor him in spite of the ways he hurt me, I began to experience God's provision on a different level. For years, I carried the burden of having to be my own provider. And as I mentioned earlier, I held that against my father. Most of my peers had never worked, but I had worked practically all of my life. Compared to others, my journey seemed to be disastrous rather than developmental. How often do we too wrongly conceptualize God's development within us as disaster? ***Comparing ourselves to other people will always deceive us into jealousy, hate, and animosity.*** When I became a little older and experienced more, I realized why God gave me the path He did. God was intentional with every job and every church I ever worked for because those were the places where God divinely placed specific people just for me. ***The more we walk in forgiveness, honor, and appreciation, the more God provides for us in a supernatural way.***

The point I am making is, you have to learn to honor and appreciate people that you do not necessarily like, people you feel do not deserve honor, and people who fail to honor and appreciate you. Now, I know you might think I'm crazy, but I have continuously won by treating people the way God commands us. My motto is: ***"The better you treat people, the better your life will be."*** Honor and appreciation unlock God's abundance. They enable us to live a life that impacts other lives and changes generations to come. I have been given opportunities I do not deserve or qualify for. I have experienced acceleration solely due to showing honor and appreciation. Honor and appreciation are attributes that have the power to change the trajectory of your life. Stop worrying about the responses of others and outdo them in showing love and honor. I know it can be tempting to want payback when people have gone out of their way to offend you. In the words of Michelle Obama, "When they go low, we go high." ***The worst part about choosing to respond in the same the way our enemies respond is that we have to become like them to do it.*** Know that people often deflect what they do not have the maturity or strength to inspect. Don't create a habit of holding on to the doubts, fears, and hurt of others. You cannot allow such little things to occupy the space God needs to prepare you for what He has already predestined. If you truly want to experience the life of abundance God has promised us, ***you must learn to honor and appreciate what God values most, His people. The next season of your life is not predicated on your willingness to work and win, but on your willingness to love limitlessly.***

" Be thankful in all circumstances,
for this is God's will for you who belong
to Christ Jesus "
(1 Thessalonians 5:18 NLT).

We have to learn to equally appreciate seasons, moments, and transitions in our lives. I have been guilty of complaining about getting up in the mornings for work instead of thanking God that I have a job where I can earn a living. Depression, anxiety, and feelings of hopelessness sometimes come from a lack of gratitude. This failure to be grateful causes us to live in regret, rather than in the beauty of redemption and restoration. ***God is not concerned with our past; neither is He living in our past, so why do we?*** Learning to thank God for everything has been life changing for me. I no longer cultivate a habit of complaining, but I have created a habit of thanking God through the good, the things my natural mind perceives as "bad," and the things over which I have no control. Appreciation is key to breaking through the boxes society often designs for us. ***Your next is determined by what you are willing to appreciate now.*** If you do not learn to value and appreciate where you are now, your next will be unattainable. Appreciation is the breeding ground for elevation. Learn to appreciate all things, people, and experiences so that your heart will be ready to receive what God has in store for you.

Is there a person or situation you can show more appreciation?

If so, how do you believe an attitude of gratitude

will make your life more enjoyable?

Who do you need to forgive?

What do you need to forgive them for?

CHAPTER 7

FORGIVENESS has always been my frailty. After encountering, as well as, witnessing so much hurt in my childhood, I decided to protect myself from any man who reminded me of the infidelity, betrayal, and downright trauma I observed as a child. As my desire for companionship increased, I started confessing, "I'm not going to jail or hell." I'm sure you find this confession comical, but it was my personal accounts that established this declaration. Forgiveness is easier in some areas than it is in others. In most instances, it can happen faster, depending on the situation and the people involved. However, when the issue revolves around the people you love the most, specifically people we refer to as family, it is as hard to forgive as it is to fold your laundry. It may never happen. In fact, you might just settle for jail or hell. Forgiveness, for me, has not been a simple concept, but implementing it has made my life easier and more enjoyable.

Forgiving family and Friends

I was twenty years old when I started dating my husband. I have literally been with him my entire adult life. Do you feel me blushing? He is four years older than me and has always remained the best boyfriend. My husband was a father before we met. Tyler, our now seventeen-year-old, was six when we started dating. My husband was not from my hometown. Therefore, no one knew anything about him. I loved this, but my mother and brothers did not. They were not comfortable with me dating an older guy who also had a child, and was out of his parents' house. That was too much for them. They responded in ways I never would have imagined. Their behavior damaged their relationship with me and their relationship with Brandon. In their quest to protect me, they hurt me. I have told them this, and we have healed. But I share this so that mistakes of this kind are not deemed normal, but unnecessary. Some thoughts, words, and deeds are simply unnecessary.

I have always been what most people would consider a "good girl." Sure, I have made my share of mistakes, but I have always been a person who delights in learning from other people's mistakes. That tendency has helped me to avoid things most people do not. While it is true that we learn from experiences, I was never the child (nor adult) to feel that everything needed to be experienced. If I knew someone who left her purse out and her money was stolen, I put my purse up. That is how I am, and I do not apologize for it! My mom had everything to do with me being this way because she has always been overly transparent about her victories and mistakes in life. She would say, "I am telling you this so you won't make the same mistake."

That was a seed that is still harvesting today. I honored and implemented her wisdom. I knew it took a lot for my mom to let me in on some of her lowest moments, but I really appreciate her doing so. I wanted my decisions and successes to be a reflection of what she had instilled in me. I was very determined for her to see that I honored her daily sacrifices. I was crushed to learn that she did not see my results! Well, at least to me, she didn't. She decided to believe that I was crazy, 'hot in the tail," and disobedient just because my man was breathtakingly handsome. Haha! Lo (Lorene) really showed out about her now son-in-law who, by the way, she now likes more than me. Moms are hilarious, right?

Anyway, it hurt. It hurt to see my family mistreat and judge someone who was so kind to me. So respectful. So humble. He was so humble that he never retaliated against their attacks, threats, or mean jokes. He refused to respond because his respect for me was greater than my family's disrespect toward him. This is where Brandon and I differ. I am "about that life" when I feel disrespected. Brandon, however, has taught me how to chill out, think, and respond later *if* it is necessary to respond. That word "necessary" keeps coming up. I am not sure why, but I trust the Holy Spirit. Let's define it.

Necessary

required to be done, achieved, or present; needed; essential.

How often do we really say, do, and think necessary things? How often do we say, do, and think *unnecessary* things? It is fair to say most of us probably do more of the unnecessary than what is actually necessary, and it is stifling to the development of our relationships. Many people fail to cultivate meaningful bonds with others due to their inability to recognize what is and is not necessary and/or dishonor the boundaries of others. Sadly, most of us would rather be committed to strife, pride, and bitterness more than authentic relationships with the very thing God uses the most--people! Further, we blame others for our poor responses in disagreements because we do not like to face the facts of our insecurities. Let me explain.

When I began dating Brandon, I experienced betrayal and lies like never before. It was not until after I started dating him that I learned you do not necessarily have to bother people for them to bother you. No, really, people truly don't need a reason to hate. Well, maybe I should say, people do not need a valid reason to hate you. Sometimes, it is more convenient for people to attack you than it is for them to attack what is really attacking them—their insecurities. Brandon and I battled opinions and slander on a daily basis. I was not as strong as him. He was raised as a pastor's kid, so he had mastered not caring about what people think. I, however, was the kind of person who always needed to make sense of things, failing to realize that some things will not make sense because they come from people who are not the (most?) sensible. Honestly, I still find myself trying to make sense of some things. When I realize I am attempting to make sense of insensible things, I pause and pray.

I am learning that I can still be a reflection of Jesus even if I decide to disconnect from people who do not contribute to the calling God has on my life. Before I accepted this truth, I struggled with the guilt of leaving people I knew in a sense needed me. I was the stronger friend, the prayer partner, and the safe space, but I had to learn that my investments are valuable. I am an asset. When people refuse to place value on the relationship and assets you offer them, you will find yourself building them while they are stripping you. Disconnection, to me, is the best opportunity to reflect the love of God. For the strong friends who struggle with letting go of people because you know they have relied on your strength, know that your distance does not mean God will distance Himself from them. It is *His* strength that is made perfect in their weaknesses, not yours. In most cases, their weaknesses end up wounding people like us because we fail to guard our hearts (Proverbs 4:23 NLT). To settle for poor relationships rather than pursue relationships that are rich in love, respect, and honor is not an act of compassion. This posture does not make you selfless. Taking this posture instead does not mean you will have first dibs at a seat beside Jesus in heaven.

To pursue people who constantly reject us simply means we long for acceptance, and that is a devastating place to live in. You deserve to be in relationships that make you feel good. You do not have to accept relationships that make you feel used, small, and drained just because you are a Christian. You can have compassion and love for people without having them in your personal inner circle. It took me a while to get here, If I am completely honest, this chapter of my life has shocked me. I have always been the girl who feels guilty when I separate myself from people I believe (in a sense) need me. Lately, I have asked myself, "They may need me, but do they deserve me?" When you are genuinely kind and intentional about how you treat people, it can be difficult to forgive when your character has been attacked, when people you really love treat you a certain way simply because you broke the box they put you in (exceeded their expectations), and having people upset with you because you disagree with them.

I recently decided that I could no longer allow the complexities of my belief to keep me in relationships that drain me of my joy. I don't care who it is or the role they play in my life. If it does not lift me, I am leaving it! Believers, hear me when I say this, your decision to not remain in relationship with people is not an act of unforgiveness. Proverbs 4:23 (NLT) says, "Guard your heart above all else, for it determines the course of your life." The results of your life are predicated on your ability to guard what you do and with whom you do it! It is not about cutting people off, but more so about understanding where they belong. With some people, the only way to guard your heart is to completely deny them access. With others, guarding your heart may look like new boundaries or limited access. Either way, it is your responsibility to determine the course of your life. God gives our lives promise and purpose, but it is up to us whether or not we show up to receive the promise by walking in the purpose. ***We, especially Christians, have to understand that we can make the love we have available to everyone while also recognizing that we are not assigned to everyone.*** Your decisions about relationships should not be made from a place of guilt, revenge, or the need to have a sense of belonging, but in the wisdom to guard your heart.

Accepting Responsibility for My Response

Believe it or not, I grew up being a horrible friend. As I mentioned, my brothers were my first friends, and they were not very good friends. They hit me for no reason. They urinated on the toilet seats. They were nasty, and real friends are not nasty! I loved them, but I developed an aggression toward them because it was the only way I knew how to survive being the only girl. Basically, I decided if they were afraid of me, they would do as I said. For the most part, that tactic worked at home, but I was not able to control the dynamics of my relationships in the real world. In my friendships with others, I quickly learned that aggression was not normal, nor was it welcoming. I became better at being relational, but I do not think I learned how to really "friend" until I met Brandon. I owe my transformation from "Trigger" Trin to "Your Friend" Trin to him.

We shared many highs and a few lows while dating. Brandon greeted both the highs and lows with the same humility and grace. I, however, was a runner. If something challenged my comfort back then, you could count me out. I did not want to find or make a way unless it was the way out. I was used to things going my way, being on my terms, and controlling the circumstances. Say you are spoiled without saying you're spoiled, right? Yes, I know. It has not always been the accountability for me.

Thankfully, Brandon was there to teach me the importance of healthy communication. Learning how to "friend" with him brought a significant increase of peace and pleasure in my relationship with him and with others. Finally, I could see how my subpar communication skills had played a major role in the emotional distance that prevailed in all of my relationships. My words and actions had to align and be a reflection of one another for my love to be received. I expected Brandon to love me because I was loyal, genuine, and thoughtful. Although he loved all of those characteristics, he needed to know that, as my friend, if he fell short, my character would remain the same. That is where I struggled. If I believed for a moment that a person was attempting to cross me, all bets were off. Here is the thing I have learned from friendship: you learn the most about your own character when you are in a state of offense.

Offense

annoyance or resentment brought about by a perceived insult to or disregard for oneself or one's standards or principles

Oftentimes, we perceive offense as the exposure of another person's character, but your character is actually exposed when you respond to offense. I thought I was a pretty good person, and I was to an extent. But I did not want to continue having limitations on my ability to "friend" when I was offended. The work is ongoing, but I have changed in ways I never could have imagined without first surrendering my poor understanding of relationship to God. God used the person closest to me to reveal the power of relationship. My ability to now be vulnerable, transparent, as well as accountable, has changed the trajectory of my life.

These attributes, alone, have changed not only who I am in relationships, but also with whom I am able to connect. We have all heard the cliché, "It is all about who you know." I have lived for over 30 years, and I have yet to see this statement return void. Who you know, who you are in relationship with, and who you have maintained the same character with overtime is pivotal to ongoing success. You will also learn that it is not always who you know, but who knows you, which is why it is important for us to build good character. I am reminded of Joseph, the dreamer.

A Story of Forgiveness

In Genesis 37, you will find the story of Joseph. Because he was born when his father, Jacob, was an old man, Joseph was Jacob's favorite son. Joseph's brothers were jealous of the bond he and Jacob shared. They envied Joseph after he confided in them about the dreams he had. These dreams revealed that he would become their leader and reign over them. I believe Joseph shared these dreams with them out of shock and a desire to understand what the dreams meant, not to make them jealous. His brothers, however, did not consider his intent, so they planned to murder him because they could not bear the thought of submitting to the leadership of Joseph, the baby of the family.

Pause. ***Learn to accept that some people will most likely see you how they've always seen you.*** To take offense about this simply means you are not ready to lead. There will always be people who discredit the calling God has on your life. Because Satan uses distractions to steal, kill, and destroy, these kinds of insults normally come from the people closest to you. As I continue to breakdown the story, you will find Joseph persevering in his purpose despite how people perceived him. That is what we should also do when people do not see what we see! Their lack of vision is not an attack against our vision. It is confirmation that they are not the people God has assigned to help you carry out the vision. I don't often suggest "clapbacks" for people because it requires too much energy, but since you are my friend, and I want you to stay focused, hand them this book so I can say it for you.

Dear family member or friend, Heaven does not hold conference calls when God calls significant people to execute His plan in this earth. You don't have to understand because you, my friend, were not on the call. Celebrate the people you love and pray for them. Discounting their abilities does not limit them; it limits you. *inserts scripture*

Your Friend,

Trin

One time for the protective people who do not play about their friends! I am you and you are me. Ha! Okay, back to Joseph.

Jacob, Joseph's father, would often send him to check on his older brothers while they were out in the field working. The brothers deeply hated this because Joseph would do just as his father requested by reporting exactly what was happening in the field. One day, as Joseph approached his brothers in the field, they began to make a mockery of him by saying, "Here comes Joseph, the dreamer." Pause. May our dreams be so big that people think we are crazy and laugh at us! When I reflect on people who were laughed at in the Bible, their results always shut the mouth of every naysayer! Don't believe me? Take some time to read not only about Joseph, but Moses, David, and Jesus! Luke 8:52-55 (NIV) reads, "Meanwhile, all the people were wailing and mourning for her. 'Stop wailing,' Jesus said. 'She is not dead but asleep.' They laughed at him, knowing that she was dead. But he took her by the hand and said, 'My child, get up!' Her spirit returned, and at once she stood up. Then Jesus told them to give her something to eat." If they laugh, it is a good sign that you are about to be lifted! I love how God orchestrates His Word. ***Where there is a laugh, there is also a lifting.*** Joseph's brothers plotted to kill him but refrained from doing so and decided to sell him into slavery to a group called the Ishmaelites. The Ishmaelites took Joseph to Egypt where his lifting would come to pass.

Genesis 39

The Bible repeatedly says that God was with Joseph, and His presence was evident through Joseph's continual lifting. Potiphar, an Egyptian officer, made Joseph his personal attendant. If I could compare his job to a job of today's society, I would describe Joseph as the Central Operating Office of Potiphar's company. Joseph had complete access to everything and succeeded in all that he did. Potiphar had no worries because God blessed his home for Joseph's sake. Of course, Satan is always seeking whom he may devour (1 Peter 5:8 KJV). He has no power to cause anything to happen, but he presents temptations for us to fall once we have been lifted. ***Your happiness, peace, and success are no benefit to Satan. He will always try to tempt you to believe he can satisfy you better. The worse off you are, the better you fit his plans to steal, kill, and destroy you and everything God has for you.***

The Bible describes Joseph as a well-built and handsome man. Potiphar's wife found Joseph attractive and would often offer him sex. He declined the offer because he knew it would be a great sin and he refused to break Potiphar's trust in him. Joseph may have been tempted considering the circumstances, but he remained true to his good character. Since we are highlighting Joseph's character, let's define what character means.

Character

the mental and moral qualities distinctive to an individual

Joseph's desire to please God was evident in his character even when his circumstances were unfair. Whenever Potiphar was away, his wife continued to harass and demand that Joseph sleep with her. One day, Joseph went into work and they were there alone. She tried once again, aggressively snatching his garment. Joseph ran out of the room and away from the house, leaving his garment in her hand. Potiphar's wife was furious that he would not have sex with her, so she lied and told the servants that Joseph attempted to rape her and ran away. Pause. ***When people don't get what they want, they will lie. Expect it so it is easier to forgive it.*** I assume this lie was her way of getting ahead of Joseph possibly telling his side of the story. When Potiphar learned of his wife's accusations, he was livid, and threw Joseph into prison. But even in prison, God remained with Joseph.

" But the Lord was with Joseph in the prison

and showed him his faithful love.
And the Lord made Joseph a favorite
with the prison warden "
(Genesis 39:21 NLT)

Let's declare this, ***"Even when my circumstances are unfair, I am favored by God."*** I believe God favored Joseph because Joseph's words and actions were a representation of good character. His circumstances were unfortunate and underserved, yet he remained true to the vision God had given him. He understood his assignment was greater than the adversity he faced. In Genesis 41, Joseph interpreted the dreams of two inmates Pharaoh had sent to the prison where the warden had appointed Joseph as a manager. Pharaoh's cupbearer happened to be one of the people who had been sent to prison and had a dream interpreted by Joseph while he was incarcerated. After the cupbearer was later released from the prison and returned to work, Pharaoh told the cupbearer that he was having dreams that he was unable to interpret. The cupbearer mentioned Joseph and how he had interpreted his dreams during his time in prison. He explained that Joseph told him he would be released from prison and return to his job as Pharaoh's cupbearer. The cupbearer's dream had come to pass, and Pharaoh was witnessing it! Therefore, the cupbearer suggested to Pharaoh that he should allow Joseph to interpret his dream.

*" Pharaoh sent for Joseph at once,
and he was quickly brought from the prison.
After he shaved and changed his clothes,
he went and stood before Pharaoh.
Then Pharaoh said to Joseph,
'I had a dream last night, and no one here can
tell me what it means. But I have heard that
when you hear about a dream you can interpret it.'
'It is beyond my power to do this,'
Joseph replied.
'But God can tell you what it means
and set you at ease' "*
(Genesis 41:14 NLT)

Let's talk CHARACTER! Joseph is saying that he is not allowed to take credit for the gift God gave him. Most people would take a moment like this to exalt themselves, but Joseph realized that, in his case, humility was the only way to break the curse of captivity. Joseph was likely tired, frustrated, and disappointed with Potiphar's previous decision to send him to prison, but he showed up anyway for God to work through him. Perhaps Joseph thought how could someone request his presence now after he had been basically thrown away, but Joseph did not let any of his emotions control his response. Instead, he allowed the love of God to prevail. His decision to choose love, honor, and obedience when he had every reason not to is why he was favored by God. Neither Joseph's appearance, personality, nor his financial status got him into the same room as Pharaoh. It was his character that caused the cupbearer to mention him. I have another question because real friends ask questions. Is your character, alone, enough to put your name in the ears of the very people who could change your life? Joseph could have been in the prison quiet, upset, or downright mean, and it would have been justifiable considering that he was put there unfairly. Instead, he maintained good character. Joseph understood his emotions were valid, but a foolish response was not. ***In confusion, good character can exist. In disappointment, good character can exist.*** In disrespect, good character can exist. Imagine if Joseph had given into temptation and slept with Potiphar's wife. He would have probably been killed and never received the manifestation of God's promise. Friend, it is not worth it. Nothing is worth forfeiting the promises of God.

" Pharaoh said to Joseph, 'I hereby put you in charge of the entire land of Egypt' "

(Genesis 41:41 NLT)

If your character shifts when your circumstances shift, you will always find yourself emotionally and mentally unstable. Because Joseph remained confident in God when he could not be confident in anything else, he thrived in captivity. He remained sane when he should have gone crazy. He remained peaceful although he was in a chaotic situation. Joseph did not allow his sentencing to steal his opportunity to display the goodness of God, which was the very thing that ended up lifting him out of captivity. Do you ever pause in times of frustration or confusion to think, "This is an opportunity for me to display the goodness of God?" Joseph used his gift even when the very people to whom he had shown nothing but commitment, honor, and loyalty had written him off. Hear me when I say this: "Don't allow offense to weaponize the gift God has given you. What if God wants to use what He has given you to set you free of the chains that people and society have placed on you? No matter what it looks like, your gift is not a weapon against you or anyone else but a tool to be used by God for His glory and for your elevation.

Maybe you are like Joseph and the enemy has been telling you that this is the end. It is not. It is actually the beginning of a new reality. Let me clarify. God's will is becoming your reality! The enemy meant the recent situations you have encountered for disaster, but God meant it for development. Be mindful that there is a place already prepared for you. God is just preparing you for it. I know I have shared bits and pieces of my childhood throughout this book, but if I could have another moment of transparency, I will tell you how God prepared me for my assignment.

How I know Joseph is my 444th cousin-

In high school, I can remember comparing my friends' families to mine. It seemed as if they were further ahead of me because they had what I believed to be functional families—two-parent homes, college-educated parents, and parents who were committed to investing in their children's lives by exposing them to more than our small-town mentality. I was not jealous, but I did wish I had more functionality. I prayed for it. I lived for it. I made all my decisions with one thought: "I do not want to live my entire life in dysfunction." Without ever blaming my parents and settling for a life God had not predestined for me, I applied what my mother had instilled in me from a very young age. She would admonish me, "Life is all about the choices you make.". This was the title of her sermon for all of my teenage years. I had heard it over and over again, but the Holy Spirit would regularly interrupt my temptations with my mother's voice of wisdom. I did not always get it right, but by the grace of God, I yielded in a lot of those moments.

I worked hard to build my character because I was determined to dismantle every label that people in our town had placed on my family. Like Joseph,

I did not allow my circumstances to limit my ability to change. I decided at an early age not to worry about what my father or anyone else would not do for me. I hustled, selling cookies at the Saturday morning rummage sales, and eventually ended up serving as a paid musician for local churches. When I turned 16, I worked at a shoe store, and, sometimes, overnight at McDonalds to make ends meet. I refused to be a burden on my mom who had to deal with the crumbled pieces my father left behind for her to put back together. I additionally did not want to burden my older brothers who were figuring life out for themselves and their families. My family has always been willing and ready to help me, but God strengthened me with good old-fashioned grit that would not allow me to depend on anyone else but Him.

My family admired this staunch work ethic and continued to encourage my hard work. I had grown so strong in the area of independence. But I was severely weakened in the areas of obedience and respecting authority. I think this was due to my independence because I never had to ask anyone for much. I did not understand why I responded to correction the way I did as a child until one day I burst into tears while talking to my god-brother, Terrance. I remember explaining how I felt like everybody expected something from me but gave me nothing. Most of my responses came from a place of anger because, even though I was proud to be an independent young woman, I often resented my "why." I rebutted everyone's attempts to correct me in moments where I needed correction because I was mad at the people giving me correction. If for a moment I thought I would survive, I would have said, "Y'all proud of me because I have figured out how to survive y'all's poor decisions not realizing this is not how a child's life is supposed to be." But I knew I would not survive (LOL)!

I always received applause for my hard work, but I was often tired. I felt like I could do better in school without so much responsibility. I wished my stepdad and my mom had never fallen out because he relieved so much of my fear and financial burdens, but he left, too. For years, I felt like the hand I had been dealt was unfair, but like Joseph, God was preparing me to prevent, protect, and preserve! This one is for the leaders of the family.

" 'I am Joseph'! he said to his brothers.
'Is my father still alive?' But his brothers were speechless!
They were stunned to realize that
Joseph was standing there in front of them.
'Please, come closer,' he said to them.
So, they came closer. And he said again,
'I am Joseph, your brother, whom you sold
into slavery in Egypt. But don't be upset,

and don't be angry with yourselves for selling me to this place. It was God who sent me here ahead of you to preserve your lives' "

(Genesis 45:3-5 NLT)

I guess you have been wondering when we would get to the "F" word? Forgiveness. Forgiveness has to be one of the most difficult things we will ever encounter. I think Satan tricks us this way because he knows that on the other side of forgiveness is an even bigger "F" word: Freedom! What I find to be most interesting about forgiveness is we rarely have to forgive people we do not know. It is the people closest to us who cause us to stumble in this area. Because who else could be such a great distraction to us, right?

In times of development, the enemy will take his opportunity to steal your NEXT by persuading you that canceling the people who have hurt you NOW will make your next better. Let me tell you this, friends. There is not a now or next without real forgiveness. ***Unforgiveness incarcerates vision and hinders creativity. When you are holding on to things that hinder your thoughts, you will always have to wait and hope to be next because now is only available to people who are ready to forgive NOW.*** Do you think Joseph would have been able to thrive in captivity and eventually land a position of leadership in the very land where he had been WRONGLY held captive if he had not forgiven his family? He did not let his brothers' offenses distract him. Joseph had a dream; and that dream, alone, was enough for him to trust God when he could no longer trust the people closest to him. Joseph was favored because he was willing to forgive. God does not lift people who want revenge.

" Blessed are the merciful,
for they shall receive mercy "
(Matthew 5:7 ESV)

Now, let's sit in the hot seat! Like Joseph's brothers, many of us allow our insecurities to end relationships with the very people God sent to lift us. Offense is inevitable in all relationships. It happens, but offense is not a reason to cancel people. Offense is, however, an opportunity to get to know people better. In the alternative perspective, it is how we respond in offense that ultimately predicates what our results will be in those relationships. Everyone experiences offense, but not everyone elevates from it. One way to grow in offense is to expect it. Offense happens when you share the vision God has given you! Everybody will not understand, but we are called to execute the plan not prosecute the people who do not understand it. ***Learn to forgive quickly because your ability to access the promises of God depends on your ability to possess the heart of God.***

Prior to meeting Brandon, dysfunctional was the only way I knew how to describe relationships, especially the ones I had experienced. I knew that, romantically, I wanted the opposite of what I grew up around, but because I had never experienced it, the introduction to it scared me. Like many people, I believed that relationships were just plain hard. I would regularly go against Brandon when he would expose me to a new way of communication and conflict resolution. This was not because I enjoyed confrontation, but because I truly did not know any better. I was subject to believing the infamous quote, "Relationships are hard." My responses were a reflection of my belief.

Thank God for exposure to not only a better way of thinking but a better way of living! My family shared the same brokenness. I grew up watching my mother avoid confrontation and my brothers overreact to confrontation. As a family, our communication skills were not healthy. I think we were so accustomed to broken communication, that healthy communication made all of us cautious of anyone who talked too good. I, however, was curious, curious to know something I had never known. That meant I had to do what I had never done, and go against what my family wanted for me. They were protective and thought like many people think—one way! I was a 20ish-year-old woman. That meant Brandon could get me pregnant. He could beat me. He could leave me. He could manipulate me and, ultimately, hold space in my life to which he had not necessarily earned the right. Friends, if I can just be transparent for a moment, I don't think it ever entered their minds that Brandon also could help me obtain what I had actually aimed for my entire life—a rich and satisfying life. For a while, I resented them for this, but the Holy Spirit revealed to me that it was my assignment to break the curse.

I have always felt like my life was an assignment. As a child, I frequently wondered, how is it that I am the only girl? How is it that I seem to be the only one who actually listens to my mama, and applies it? I wondered if my siblings honored the sacrifices my mother had made for us. As a teenager, I found myself equally motivated and irritated by my family's results with relationships in and outside of our home. I knew my purpose was to expose my family to healthy relationships. My choice to be with Brandon was not the start. The start was actually going against their judgments to create something I had yet to see in our family—*peace*. This is where I see myself in Joseph's story! I started by changing my perspective about Brandon. I realized I had to be willing to go against them to help them realize there is more to life, ***and that just because people are different from you does not mean that they are bad people.***

I strongly felt that, with Brandon, I could grow to be more than I had set out to be because he was constantly pushing me. Even in my uncertainty, I was determined not to let my family's uncertainty limit my ability to create a life I had not known, but had vividly envisioned. Maybe Brandon could be good for me. Maybe his upbringing in a stable, two-parent household could be beneficial to my lack thereof. Perhaps, him having a son was an opportunity for me to grow in love and selflessness. And maybe, he wanted something I had been groomed to be all of my life—a wife who was God-fearing, self-sufficient, and understood her self-worth. I would add value to him, and he would add value to me. Because I had grown up in what I like to call developmental circumstances, I had self-love and confidence that could not easily be stripped away from me. Although my family had highlighted what they believed to be my weaknesses, I decided to date with my strengths, rather than my weaknesses.

As I mentioned, I was far from a perfect girl, but I was a fairly good girl. I had a desire to please God at a young age, and it was evident in my decisions as well as my results. I was BLESSED. Unfortunately, brokenness is such a commonality in the black community that we sometimes place a side-eye on anything that looks or has the potential to be whole. When I say whole, I mean no missing pieces. Some of us subconsciously believe certain people and things are just too good to be true. I have worked tirelessly to shatter that belief. Life is a beautiful gift and to experience the beauty of it, you must be intentional about seeing it as a gift. How do you treat gifts? Do you just throw your new bag in a corner? Do you get a cake on your birthday and throw it away? NO! You cherish your gifts because you realize the gift is a reflection of what you mean to the people who give them to you. The people and circumstances in our lives are a reflection of what we mean to God!

" The thief's purpose is to steal and kill and destroy. My purpose is to give them a rich and satisfying life "

(John 10:10 NLT)

A rich and satisfying life seems like only a fantasy to people who are not willing to do the work that is necessary to access that kind of life. It is imperative that we understand the foundation of all decisions is *value*. What we truly value will always play out in our behavior toward others and our decisions in life. When we are not experiencing the beauty of life, it is because we are not making constant decisions that cause us to live the life God has promised us.

Value

a person's principles or standards of behavior; one's judgment of what is important in life

This is not something I understood when I chose my desires over my family's desires for me. At the time, all I knew was that I was curious to see if I could make the vision I had for my life a reality. I valued family, but I valued my vision more because I understood I was assigned to expose us to not only a different life but a quality life. I was assigned to break the curse of poor communication that keeps families divided. I was assigned to ask the hard questions that exposed us to ourselves. I was assigned to teach us the value of relationships with one another first. I learned that I was not just possessive or protective of my family. I had an assignment, and everything that never made much sense to me started to make all the sense in the world.

For my friends who understand assignment, value, and timing, we are not crazy; we are called. While I have been intentional about learning from other people's experiences, I have never allowed their experiences to determine what mine could be. Your life is purposed to bring God, and only God, glory. When your family is advising you, consider how the consequences of some of their decisions have truly affected you. This is a great way to determine if their advice is something you would like to decline or accept! It is good wisdom to take what is good and leave what is not. Just food for thought!

Understanding your assignment increases your ability to release emotions that do not belong to you. Let me remind you of what does belong to you.

" For God hath not given us the spirit of fear; but of power, and of love, and of a sound mind "

(2 Timothy 1:7 KJV)

Forgiving people became easier for me when I realized how much power I gave them by choosing not to forgive. Unforgiveness strips you of your power and limits your love. And you certainly do not have a sound mind when your heart is polluted because the heart and the mind are connected.

" But Jesus, knowing their thoughts, said, 'Why do you think evil in your hearts?' "

(Matthew 9:4 ESV)

I tried fake forgiveness. For instance, I still said things like, "I'll speak, but I don't have anything for them." This is the kind of false forgiveness that forfeits your assignment because you fail to realize that loving people, in spite of, is a part of every believer's assignment. ***"I got next" will forever be the declaration of a person who is not ready to forgive now.*** Forgiveness is an extension of grace, and we all need grace. To believe in God is not just the state of believing, but also the state of responding like we believe Him. Too many people see the word "believe" as a noun rather than an action word that requires us to go beyond the rules of Christianity to possess a relationship with God that reflects in all of our relationships, conversations, and even in offense. I know, I know. It is hard, but if it hurts, it heals. Forgiving them will free you to love them the way God calls us to love, and that is unconditionally! I recently asked a friend where loves comes from and she responded, "God." I replied, "Well, do we have a right to limit anything that comes from Him?" Seriously, think about it. If love comes from God and it is limitless, how can we say we love, but with limits? If it can run out, is it really love?

Not God using my advice to a friend to check me...

Here's to another moment of transparency. I know I have had a lot of these moments, but we are friends, aren't we? I often find that the Holy Spirit rebukes me with my own revelation of God's word. Before I shared this revelation with my friend, I placed significant limitations on a person who I discovered did not truly value my friendship. If you know me, you know I "friend" on another level. My friends become my family because I commit to them that way. It really hurt my feelings to have someone I know I have been good to act as if I have done the opposite of that, due to their own insecurities and trauma. How did I, the praying friend become the target?

How did I, the joyful friend, become a point of reference for their lack of joy? How did I, the cheerleader friend, become the competitive friend? For the first time in my life, I had a "friend" who was upset with me for not only getting better, but delivered. A person I loved as family questioned my happiness and progression in life as if it was too good to be true. Having these feelings deflected at me hit hard because I could not make sense of the accusations. I instantly distanced myself to avoid further harm and to keep from losing it on someone I love. I made a decision, some time ago, to treat people well, even if they don't treat me well. When I'm unsure if a person will feel the fruit of the spirit (goodness, patience, kindness, etc.) in my presence, I give myself time away from them until the fruit has overcome the flesh because the fruit of the spirit brings healing. The flesh of Trinity brings these hands, and I've told y'all I'm not going to jail or hell. When I took time to process, evaluate, and forgive, I found myself "forgiving" but finessing my new boundaries as love. It was a form of love, but self-love, not really godly love. If we are not careful, we will get caught up in the world's way of loving, instead of God's way. The world teaches us to love ourselves first. God teaches us to love Him first, and to prove our love for Him by loving our neighbors as we love ourselves. Wait! Before you close this book on me, give me a chance!

Let me simplify. We are not like the world. We do not give "energy," we give love. Energy and love are not one in the same. Energy will inevitably change, but love should not change! We modify our energy when needed, but we never modify love! I know that energy is a big word in society right now, but I strongly feel it is a trick of the enemy to distract us from real love and to keep us from possessing the fruit of the spirit. which draws people to God. This is why I will not stop preaching to GUARD YOUR HEART. Guard your heart in relationships with other people and in all aspects of life. That means guarding it on social media, when you hear the bad news about a person you do not like, and when you feel yourself locking your heart away from people you feel no longer deserve to have a relationship with you. Even if they do not deserve you, the access, energy, and boundaries may be modified in disconnection, but love and compassion have no modifications. My prayer for you, friend, is that you will embrace the beauty of forgiveness. Repudiating forgiveness says to our flesh, "You can have control of my outcome." Paul reminds us, in Romans 7:18, that there is no good thing within our flesh! After accepting my unwarranted rebuke, yet an extension of grace from the Holy Spirit, I wrote a prayer of forgiveness that would enable me to access real healing and restoration.

"A Prayer for Limitless Love"

Father, thank you for being my forever friend. Thank you for the ability to lean into Your presence and away from everything that easily besets me.

Teach me to control my thoughts when I am unable to control my circumstances. Teach me to respond only when You give me direction and not because I'm desperate to get my point across. Help me to pause, assess, and PRAY when I'm tempted to let people have it.

Father, I realize I will never be the perfect fit for anyone but you, but I also realize everyone doesn't fit the assignment and purpose You have given me. Let my heart not find offense in people's inability to see, appreciate, or value me, for I am on assignment. And the assignment is greater than the adversity I will face. Purify my thoughts and intentions so that I don't become a person who limits the unlimited. Teach me to accept accountability so that my response to others is not isolation or resentment, but kindness, acceptance, and understanding.

Reveal my true helpers, and show me who I am assigned to help. This time, I don't ask for You to remove people I don't agree with, but let the love I give be a reflection of the friendship I share with You.

Amen

Now, Not Next

Imagine it is the middle of August in Mississippi. That means the high today could be upwards of 98 to 103 degrees. It is not just hot; it is also humid. You are resting in the comfort of your home, enjoying the air conditioner and an iced tea, while avoiding the outside temperatures until around 7:00 p.m. In Mississippi, especially in the Delta region, we don't go outside until the sun starts to set. For my fellow Mississippians, I am certain this is not the same sun from the 90s when we played outside as kids from sunup to sundown.

Anyway, you are sitting in your home and, all of a sudden, everything powers off. As Mississippians, our worst fear is having a power outage on a hot summer day. It is not just about being hot, but you have a solid hour to have the power restored before everything in the refrigerator and freezer starts to thaw and spoil. Imagine waiting on Entergy or the local light company to restore the power and, during the wait, all of your food spoils. Because misery loves company, you step outside hoping to see your neighbors on their porches trying to catch a breeze, and possibly have a conversation about how unfair these circumstances are, but no one is outside. In fact, you notice that every house *except* your house has power.

You are frustrated now because you thought this outage was one you had no control over, only to realize all you had to do was flip the breaker. Four hours have gone by, you are sweaty, and your food is spoiling. You immediately rush over to the breaker box, flip the breaker, and prepare to throw out all of the food you previously bought. While throwing out your "Pick 5" deal of meat you purchased at the local market, feelings of anxiety and frustration set in because you know this loss could have easily been avoided if you had only gotten up and checked the breaker box when the outage initially happened. Sometimes, outages are okay when we are convinced that we are not experiencing the outage alone. It is not until we see other people moving in their power that causes us to think one of three things: "I wish I had that." "Success is only for the lucky ones." And the all-time favorite, "I got next."

But, my question to you is, why are you not experiencing the power now? According to 2 Timothy 1:7, the power has been distributed to all of us, not just a certain group of people. The only difference between you and the people you are witnessing is their willingness to check the breaker box. What is the breaker box? The core values we have discussed throughout this book such as appreciation and honor, love, and accountability determine the caliber of our character. ***Doing the work of building good character***

is essential to creating opportunities that ignite the power within us to make our dreams a reality NOW.

The promise is available to all of us, but few people are willing to disintegrate the parts of our character that challenges us to get into the position that is necessary to receive it. The food did not just thaw and spoil because the power went out; it thawed and spoiled because you were comfortable laying on the couch, scrolling through social media, and sipping tea until you started to smell your groceries going to waste! We often assume that we have to wait for help when all we need to do is get up! Once you get up, you will discover that you have everything you need to create a new reality. We already have the power to access the life God intended for us to have. And that life is available to us now, not next, but this God-kind-of-life requires fortified faith that does not merely exist but executes the vision God has for our lives.

" 'You don't have enough faith,' Jesus told them. 'I tell you the truth, if you had faith even as small as a mustard seed, you could say to this mountain, "Move from here to there," and it would move. Nothing would be impossible' "

(Matthew 17:20 NLT)

What does it mean to have faith? Is it really a matter of having just enough that is as small as a mustard seed? Let me just be honest. I believe it is time we extirpate the theory that mustard seed faith is all you need to see miracles manifested in your life. Jesus was not telling the disciples that faith the size of a mustard seed was all they needed. He was rebuking them for not having enough faith, not even faith as small as a mustard seed! What I'm saying is, the seed is where our faith starts, not where it ends! Now, I know most of us have heard all we need is mustard seed faith all of our lives, but since Jesus used the analogy of faith being the size of a mustard seed, let's define and learn the purpose of a seed.

Seed

a flowering plant's unit of reproduction,

capable of developing into another such plant

As believers, we must understand that God expects everything He gives us to grow. For instance, we were all seeds before we were growing fetuses in our mothers' wombs, and we were fetuses before we were babies. The sole purpose of a seed is to proceed into its next stage until it is fully developed. Everything in life, including faith, has developmental stages. Since we are discussing seeds, do you remember how many stages a seed has to go through before it is fully developed? Google it. I'll wait.

I had hoped to find seven stages, compare it to the spiritual meaning of completion, and go into a preaching frenzy about the process to completion concerning faith, but I found only six stages. After speculating for a moment, I came to the conclusion that God has no intention for our faith to finish, but to continuously flourish. Flourishing faith requires obedience and submission to the real will of God for our lives. Yes, I said real because many of us would rather convince ourselves that our own will is God's will. The reality is that you cannot finesse the will of God. We get to decide whether we want the will of God to be manifested in our lives, but we do not, however, get to decide the process of manifestation. When we try to dictate our process, we find ourselves feeling overwhelmed and confused about what God has given us to do.

We have witnessed those people who change their purpose anytime something does not go the way they expected. I have been guilty of suggesting that my will is God's because I was either afraid I would not like His will or afraid I would disappoint my family who thought my life was a pretty good life. Being thought of as ungrateful when you are actually tired of being stagnant can be difficult because you know your family wants what is best for you, but at the same time, their best does not remotely compare to God's best. I am still learning to allow my family and closest friends to protect me without subjecting me to lives they prefer.

Where I come from, a $35K annual income is phenomenal. If you can get your bills paid without having to ask anyone to borrow money until your next paycheck, you are "balling". My life was comfortable, and for years, I had fulfilled the desires everyone else had for me, and none of my own desires. Because I grew up in developmental circumstances, having a secure job with benefits provided me with the life for which my mother often hoped. "I just want to be comfortable" were her words anytime the conversation pertained to money and finances.

In retrospect, I feel like I became bound to living a life that would please her, not me. Because she had made so many sacrifices for me, I felt like I owed it to her to not only do well but to do it exactly how she had advised me to, even if that meant teaching for thirty plus years and retiring. To be honest, I loved teaching, but I never wanted to teach. I was playing it safe because all my life, that is what I had been taught to do. Not to mention, this safety provided me with a comfortable lifestyle. I could not do much more than pay bills, but I could do that without asking anyone for help. I had "arrived" at a place my family and close friends considered successful. I did, too, but I always felt this nudging in my heart that I was diminishing the assignment God had for my life. I wanted my seed to prosper in a place in which I had never been called to plant.

Education fit me well, and I became comfortable with holiday and summer breaks. I started to plan pregnancies and my life around my job. ***My comfort had become my crisis because I was stuck trying to make this place of development my final destination.*** Yes, my calling involved teaching, but I was not seeking God for instruction before I started this journey. I was seeking validation from the people closest to me. I wanted to be sure they felt like I was doing something with my life, even if that meant I had to settle for a life I did not really want. When we are not truly submitted to the will of God, we will subconsciously mistake our desire to be validated for God's instruction. I really did love God and desired to do the right things. Therefore, I assumed I would be rewarded. I have finally grown to realize that being or doing right is not a substitution for obedience. Sure, I would often be rewarded with Teacher of the Month and receive frequent gifts for my commitment to the profession, but it was not changing my life. I had to face the reality that I was serving Jehovah Jireh, the God of more than enough, and I was not living a life that reflected that because I only had enough. Having a real life-change is not in doing the "right" thing but in being obedient to the will of the Lord. From this experience, I have learned to prioritize two things:

1. Alignment and
2. Assignment

The things we consider "right" do not always align with our God-given assignments. For example, millions of people have accumulated debt for degrees they have barely or never used in the name of doing the "right" thing. Or like me, we find ourselves feeling like misfits years after we have committed to a particular profession before we realized our purpose is not in a certain profession but in our alignment with the will of God for our lives. Following systems of the world can be detrimental to our divine destiny. I am not saying all the "right" things should not be done, or systems should not be followed, but the Bible says in Matthew 6:33 (NLT), "Seek the kingdom of God above all else, and live righteously, and he will give you everything you need." This means that God wants to be our greatest desire first, and everything else we desire will be given to us. We are not called to follow the systems of the world but the system of the kingdom, which is seeking God first, living righteously, and knowing that as we seek Him, He adds *everything* that we need. Not some things, but *everything*. That includes direction and instruction (Proverbs 3:5-6).

Some people find virtues like perseverance, hope, and faith useless. They believe what is meant for you will eventually come to you. That is not the way it works though! Being content with never having to believe God for more is not a flex. It is not proof that you are grateful, but it is proof that you are not in pursuit of your purpose. To avoid believing is also to avoid the abundant life to which God has called you. Y***ou will always have to hope to be next when you are underserving of experiencing the supernatural life NOW.*** One day, I was tired of doing just better than good. Settling for the systems of the world not only deferred the evolution of my faith, but for some time, it robbed me of my future. When I trusted God fully, I started to explore ideas I had never before been able to conceive. It changed my conversations, my work ethic, but most of all, my ability to create.

Perhaps your faith has remained the size of a mustard seed because you have not given it a reason to grow. Friend, I want you to know this. Living a life that requires little to no faith is NOT the will of God, for the Bible tells us that without faith, it is impossible to please God (Hebrews 11:6 ESV)! God has a plan for you, and it requires your faith to flourish. Faith does not flourish when there is no adversity attached to it. Faith flourishes in the face of adversity because adversity requires the belief to overcome.

The Holy Spirit has revealed to me that you have been dodging your adversity, but you should know that your assignment is greater than the adversity you will face. The adversity is simply preparation for what God has already done for us. There is no promise without the process. When you accept the call God has on your life, you must also accept the development that comes with it. David was crowned king while he was yet a shepherd boy working in the field, but in that field, he developed the skills that were necessary to later defeat Goliath. His promise was to be king, but his process made him one of the greatest warriors and worshipers in scripture.

Accepting that there is no evolution without execution is key to breaking the code that often confines us to one place and profession in life. God wants us to live a life that reflects His goodness, abundance, and character. ***If your faith does not grow, neither will you.*** Playing it safe may be serving your current circumstances, but because there is greater within you, God is going to constantly shift your circumstances until He is able to shift you. PSA: You have not been under attack. You have been in divine development. No longer will you underestimate the power of your faith. ***God is saying to you, the time is NOW.***

We've all heard the story about the woman with the issue of blood. For twelve years, she lived with this condition, and one day, she decided that the time was NOW. My Pastor, Dr. Kellie Agueze, often says, "Everything starts with a decision." I could not agree more. The woman with the issue of blood knew that Jesus was passing by, so she made a decision to be freed of her condition.

" For she thought to herself,
'If I can just touch his robe, I will be healed' "
(Mark 5:28 NLT)

This woman had seen doctor after doctor, and none of them had given her a remedy. Imagine bleeding for twelve years in a world where innovative feminine products are yet to exist. She was considered unclean and probably had a foul odor that made her embarrassed to be around others. This condition had robbed her of twelve years, but finally she decided to MOVE. Remember when I told you earlier that God is always moving and that we also have to move for our faith to collide with his power? The woman with the issue of blood knew that Jesus was passing by, so she pressed her way through a crowd of thousands of people. This woman understood the assignment! She did not allow the process to paralyze her faith. She believed, and her response was a reflection of how big her belief was.

Pressing through that crowd to touch Jesus was not little faith; it was desperate faith. Have you ever lost someone, specifically a child, in a huge crowd after a concert or ball game? The desperation to find them causes you to maneuver through that crowd in a way that you never would have if you were not desperate. The circumstances we sometimes encounter are not only meant to teach us to depend on God, but God allows them to make us desperate for Him. Because God is a jealous God, He does not want us to count on our own abilities and resources, He wants to be our first and last resort. In order for that to happen, He has to allow us to see that He is our greatest source and not merely one of our resources.

In adversity, our desperation for deliverance grows. The fact that the woman with the issue of blood had seen multiple doctors over a course of twelve years lets us know that her faith flourished through her adversity. Notice that we do not see this woman begging Jesus for a miracle. She simply believed. ***If we believe God, we don't have to beg God!*** Believing is not just a state of being, but believe is a verb that requires actions of belief. The woman with the issue of blood walked by faith, not by sight. ***She realized her healing was not in waiting, but in pursuing.*** She made up in her mind that her breakthrough would not come when or if Jesus got to her. She was BOLD! She went to Him. Her faith was so strong that Jesus stopped and asked, "Who touched my robe?" The disciples were trying to explain that the crowd was pressing against them and anyone could have touched him, but Jesus continued to look because He had felt healing virtue leave His body. Finally, the frightened woman came and admitted to touching Jesus and instantly being healed. You may be wondering why I decided to go back to this story when we have already acknowledged it. Here it is.

" And he said to her, 'Daughter, your faith has made you well. Go in peace. Your suffering is over' "

(Mark 5:34 NLT)

The impromptu opportunities presented to us are often the same opportunities that change the trajectory of our lives. The woman with the issue of blood did not know what Jesus had on His agenda that day, but she knew He was passing by, so she positioned herself to receive the miracle. In order for our faith to grow, we must get into position. ***Sometimes, the position is scary, new, and even unpopular, but we must be willing to make the miracle we need happen now, not next.*** Like the woman with the issue of blood, we should not let the crowd keep our faith from flourishing. ***Our results are our responsibility.*** We do not plant seeds, dig them up, and replace them when growth is not happening fast enough. We simply trust that if we water the seed and expose it to sunlight, it will grow.

The woman with the issue of blood was convinced that if she kept moving and was only able to touch the hem of Jesus' robe, she would be healed. It is the same for our faith. To exercise your faith, you will face things that cause you to water your seed in prayer. We will face things that make no sense—things that cause us to feel embarrassed. But you know what I have learned, Friend? ***God elevates people who are willing to be embarrassed for Him.*** He proves the doubters wrong and shuts the mouths of naysayers. Just as the woman with the issue of blood received her breakthrough after she positioned herself, God reveals His power in our positioning. ***We cannot experience the power of God before we are positioned to receive it.*** God wants us to check our breaker box. It may be frustrating and tiresome, but the sooner you check the breaker box, the sooner God can intervene on your behalf. We live in a world where everything is happening fast, and sometimes, we expect great expedition to be our portion. If that were the case, we would not appreciate or value God's timing.

" Now faith is the substance of things hoped for, the evidence of things not seen "

(Hebrews 11:1 KJV)

This is probably one of the most prominent scriptures known amongst Christians. We tend to focus on the faith element, and that is good, but the timing of our faith cannot be overlooked. God is intentional with His Word. Every word in every place is for a divine purpose. When does faith, the substance of things hoped for and the evidence of things unseen, happen? NOW. Your faith is evidence that what you have been praying and believing for has arrived. You have to move like it. Talk like it. And BE it! If you want to own a business, you have to start working your faith now even if that means waking up early and going to sleep later. What we learned from the woman with the issue of blood is that desperate faith gets God's attention. ***The result is predicated on your response.*** If you really believe in the vision God has given you, why are you procrastinating? Do you really believe the results will come if you never make a decision to start?

Believe

accept (something) as true; feel sure of the truth of

When we say we believe but remain hesitant about moving in our belief, it is a reflection of our lack of trust in God. During our morning prayer watch at work a few weeks ago, Dashaunka Cooper, better known as Auntie, said something I found to be so penetrating. She said, "You trust God naturally when you have a relationship with Him." This made me think about a father referenced in the book of Mark.

" The father instantly cried out, 'I do believe, but help me overcome my unbelief' "

(Mark 9:24 NLT)

I know many of us have moments like this where we believe, but the weight of our circumstances seems to be stronger than our belief. This feeling of unbelief should serve as a sign that we need to cultivate our relationship with God. Why should we live wondering if God can, when God WILL? The father instructed the disciples to pray, but his son remained possessed until He asked Jesus to help his unbelief. The woman with the issue of blood received her breakthrough instantly because she believed God would heal her instantly.

" What do you mean, 'If I can'?" Jesus asked. "Anything is possible if a person believes "

(Mark 9:23 NLT)

I have one more question. What is the quality of your belief? Are you wondering if God can, or are you fully convinced that He will? At times, we feel our days of thriving have not ceased when we have simply ceased to believe. The results you have experienced before now were not due to the absence of God but to the absence of faith. When Jesus compared faith to a mustard seed, He knew our faith had to be planted in the dominion and authority God gave us. It was not about having just a little faith, but *quality* faith. Quality faith believes with no doubt or uncertainty. Quality faith executes and praises God in advance for what is to come. Quality faith does not wait; it works. Quality faith expects because it executes. Even if your faith is new, once it is planted in belief and watered with work (James 2:26), it has to bear fruit that reflects the quality of faith it takes to access the life God has promised us (Luke 6:44).

" They are like trees planted along a riverbank,
with roots that reach deep into the water.
Such trees are not bothered
by the heat or worried
by long months of drought.
Their leaves stay green,
and they never stop producing fruit "
(Jeremiah 17:8 NLT)

I have fallen in love with this scripture because it reminds me not to fold when my circumstances do not look like the promise. ***For every promise, there is a process.*** Becoming a tree planted along the riverbank is our promise, but the development of our seed is the process. Mustard seed faith is not all we need, but it is the inception to not just bearing fruit but bearing fruit that is ripe. Remember when I told you that the COVID-19 breakout taught me to always be ready? I want you to really think about this. What kind of fruit do you bear? Your fruit should be ready and beneficial to those around you at all times. As your friend and accountability partner, I think it is necessary for you to create a habit of evaluating your fruit.

" For a good tree does not bear bad fruit,
nor does a bad tree bear good fruit.
For every tree is known by its own fruit.
For men do not gather figs from thorns,
nor do they gather grapes
from a bramble bush "
(Luke 6:43-44 NKJV)

It is not just the fruit of our labor, but also the fruit of our faith, that is produced when we choose to trust God in our process. You may never be perfect, but you will be prepared.

" Now unto him that is able to do exceedingly
abundantly above ll that we ask or think,
according to the power that worketh in us, "
(Ephesians 3:20 KJV)

I noted earlier that most people love Ephesians 3:20 because we highlight that God will do exceedingly, abundantly and above all we can ask or think. But for me, it is like good peach cobbler. What is the filling without the crust on the top and bottom? The first word of this scripture is NOW! Not *next* unto him, but NOW unto Him that is able to do exceedingly, abundantly above all that we ask or think, according the *power* working in us! If you have the power, you can access the "exceedingly, abundantly above all you can ask or think" NOW. You do not have to wait for your power to be restored when you have access to the breaker box. It is time for you to start working your power. For too long, you have waited in doubt that eventually turned into frustration and anger because you failed to use your power. You have fought feelings of inadequacy and even jealousy because the people around you have been moving in their power. Maybe, you have experienced a life of stagnancy because you thought you needed to wait on God to prepare you, but the actual preparation comes in WORKING, not waiting! This one is for you. It is your turn, Friend! I reassure you that you have what it takes to access the life God already prepared for you.

" For God has not given us a spirit of fear and timidity, but of power, love, and self-discipline "

(2 Timothy 1:7 NLT)

The privilege has been given to you. The power belongs to you. Preparations have been made for you. Now is the time to stop talking about next time.

Your Friend,

Trin

" See, I am sending an angel before you
to protect you on your journey
and lead you safely to the place
I have prepared for you "

(Exodus 23:20 NLT)

Limitless love is not to be mistaken for poor boundless. What boundaries could you employ to improve the way you love?

Made in the USA
Columbia, SC
07 October 2023

23951896R00100